THE WAY TO BE HAPPY!
45 Key Ways That I Know To Overcome Depression, Fear, And Guilt!

The Ways to Control Your Thoughts!

The Ways to Overcome a Quick Temper!

Ruth Henderson

GOOD NEWS PUBLICATIONS
P.O. BOX 831108
STONE MOUNTAIN, GEORGIA 30083

Dearest Reader: Please note that throughout this book, the name of satan is never capitalized, unless it is in a quote by another writer. It is not due to any grammatical error, but due to the fact that I do not want to give any honor to the devil whatsoever, not even to the point of capitalizing the first letter of his name. Also, please note that all Bible Scriptures were taken from the King James Version.

FIRST DEDICATION

This book is dedicated to the Heavenly Father, His Son, Jesus Christ, and the Comforter, the Holy Spirit!

SECOND DEDICATION

This book is also dedicated to my precious loved ones, Dontaye Wellington Henderson, Rae Gibson-Canady, Jean and Lee Joyner, Roosevelt and Judy Henderson, Cliff, Sean, Martinique, John Henderson III, Omarinika Henderson, Keith Fisher, Earline Gibson, Sarita Ward, Dawn Gibson, Brent Henderson, the Henderson's, the Jackson's, the Dudley's, and the Pitts.

HOW TO BE HAPPY
AND OVERCOME
FEAR AND DEPRESSION!

In order to run fear and depression away,
Just get down on your knees and pray.
Listen to uplifting music and sing songs of
Praise.
This will run fear and depression into their
Graves.
Call on the mighty name of Jesus Christ!
Then fear and depression will run for their lives.
Get your mind off of yourself.
Go and do good deeds to help someone else.
Then you won't have time to dwell on you;
Nor to feel afraid, or sad and blue.
Read the Bible about God's great Love.
Then fear and depression will not be thought of.
If fear and depression try to enter your mind,
Quickly reject them every single time.
Trust in God's never-failing care.
He can help you win in the battle of spiritual
Warfare.
Spend quality time on your knees.
Seeking God's presence will cause fear
And depression to flee.
Claim God's promises,
In times of need.
They will build your faith when you're weak.
You no longer have to feel fearful or depressed.
**Just do these things and you will have
Peace and Happiness!**

CONTENTS

INTRODUCTION

Depression impacts millions of people from all walks of life. According to a report from the Substance Abuse and Mental Health Services Administration, one in five Americans experienced some sort of mental illness in 2010. Depression has become our nation's number one emotional illness and it is increasing steadily. It is no mere coincidence that almost 15 million Americans suffer from depression, and that millions more are struggling to cope with some other form of emotional or mental illness.

I truly believe that our adversary, the devil, is behind much of this widespread and growing problem. The devil has had thousands of years to study the human brain and learn how to influence it, or affect it. If he can control the mind, he can control people, and so he is attacking people's minds to cause fear, guilt, discouragement, confusion, and all sorts of mental illnesses.

The devil knows that his time is short, and soon he will be destroyed when Jesus returns. Therefore, the devil is working overtime like a desperate, insane, roaring lion to harass and destroy as many of our minds as he possibly can. The devil wants to get control of our minds, so that he can get control of us.

However, we don't have to be the devil's victims. We can be victorious through the power and strength of Christ. We don't have to allow the enemy to destroy our sanity; to rob us of our happiness, or to steal our peace of mind. We need to become wise to the devil's devices and his strategies that he uses to attack us. God has not left us defenseless and alone to fight in this spiritual battle against the forces of darkness. God has given us mighty spiritual weapons to triumph in the battle over depression, fear, and spiritual warfare. Nevertheless, if we do not know what our spiritual weapons are, or if we do not know how to use them effectively, we will continue to fight a losing battle.

It is unfortunate, but many dear people have been trying to fight the spiritual battles of life by using physical weapons. Too often they have assumed that their emotional and mental illnesses are due to physical problems, so they try to use physical methods such as medication as a solution. Medication, however, can in many instances only be a temporary band-aid to medicate what may be a deeper, more serious underlying problem that stems not from a physical, but from a *spiritual nature.* This is why individuals with emotional and mental illnesses many times do not recover or get healed by using only medication, or physical means. It is because the solution to their problem is not necessarily *medication,* but *spiritual education.*

We all need to be spiritually educated to recognize when we are under the attack of the devil. We also need to be able to recognize if, in fact, it is the devil who is the one causing us to feel depressed, or fearful, or guilty. And once we determine that the devil is the real culprit, then, we need to learn what our spiritual weapons are, and how we can use them successfully to defeat the devil.

In Hosea 4:6, God declares, **"My people are destroyed for lack of knowledge."** In this book, I will attempt to give you the practical knowledge, as well as the knowledge of the "spiritual weapons" that you can use to overcome depression, fear, and guilt; and to win in the battle of spiritual warfare against the powers of darkness.

My seven-fold premises and goals for writing this book are:

1. To help you find concrete, practical ways you can be truly happy in your life.

2. To help you understand what you can do to overcome depression, fear, worry, and guilt, because these are some of the major ways that the devil uses to take control of an individual's mind; that is to work through our natural emotions and other scheming avenues.

3. To help you learn how to control your thoughts and overcome negative thinking.

4. To teach you how to recognize the devil's strategies of attack; his wiles or tricks so that you can avoid and resist them.

5. To teach you how to be truly born again, because once you have the new birth experience, this will give you Christ's supernatural power within you to overcome depression, fear, guilt, and the forces of evil.

6. To help you understand how to have an effective and improved prayer life. This will also help empower you to overcome depression, fear, guilt, and the powers of darkness, because the devil trembles when we diligently and fervently pray.

7. To equip you with seven important Key Ways to overcome a quick temper.

Chapter
1

45 Ways to Be Happy, and to
Overcome Depression!

There are some people who suffer from depression, but they don't even know that they are depressed. Based on my research, along with my own personal experience with depression, I have discovered that depression is an emotional illness which is curable. It can result from genetics and family history, environmental stress, traumatic experiences, biochemical imbalances, or personality factors. The symptoms of depression are: not sleeping, or sleeping too much, feeling down all throughout the day, having difficulty making decisions, restlessness, or slowness, finding it hard to concentrate, feeling worthless and blaming yourself too much, thinking about death and suicide too frequently, fatigue, or loss of energy almost every day, experiencing a significant change in appetite or weight, and no longer interested in favorite activities.

I have discovered that there are two types of people in the world; those who choose to be happy, and those who choose to be unhappy. Contrary to popular belief, happiness doesn't come from fame, fortune, other people, or material possessions. Rather, it comes from within, and from a heart at peace with God, the Creator. Happy people are happy because they *choose* to be happy, and they do the things that *make* themselves happy.

You can overcome depression, fear, and guilt, and begin living a happy life today! By *faith* you can move mountains! However, having a *right attitude* towards your ability to recover from any trial, any problem, or any illness is one of the key ingredients to having the victory. Starting today you can leave your fear, depression, and guilt behind, and live your life with freedom, joy and peace of mind!

It is a very sad commentary, but many of the people in the church are just as sick as the non-believers in the world. However, Christians should be in better health than non-believers, because Christians should be partaking of a healthier diet than non-believers. Yet, because many Christians eat like the world, they get the same diseases and sicknesses of the non-believers in the world. However, I will explain to you how you can eat better in order to have better health physically, mentally, and emotionally.

Below is a list of 45 vital ways I know that you can be happy, and overcome depression.

Some of them are temporary things, and some of them are long-term things you can do. So are you ready? Let's get started.

1. **Take care of your body.** Some people are depressed due to a poor diet, and their brain and body is lacking the proper nutrition. If you do not take proper care of your body, it will not function properly, and neither will your mind. We must nourish our bodies in order to nourish our minds. Some people are depressed due to an inadequate diet. What you eat has a direct impact on how you feel physically as well as mentally. Therefore, adopt healthy eating and lifestyle habits. If you take care of your body, it will take care of you. Health is not a right. Health is a privilege and a choice. You only get one body, and if you take your body for granted, you will reap what you sow in poor mental and physical health.

So how can you take care of your body?

- By making sure you eat nourishing foods, because eating the wrong kinds of foods such as junk foods can negatively affect your mood and mental function.

- By reducing your intake of sugar, and high fructose corn syrup. Some people are sugar addicts and eat too much sugar. Here are some important facts that I discovered about sugar, and that you need to be aware of. This information is by Dr. Nancy Appleton from her book *"Lick the Sugar Habit."* Dr. Appleton states that "sugar can suppress the immune system, sugar upsets the minerals in the body, sugar can cause kidney damage, sugar can cause migraine headaches, sugar weakens eyesight, sugar can cause cataracts, sugar can cause Candida albicans, (yeast infections), and so forth."

I use as little sugar as possible, and if I use it at all, I use brown sugar because it has not been bleached to make it white. It still has some of the nutrients in it, but I prefer to use honey, or maple syrup, or truvia because these are natural sweeteners without the chemicals and drug content. I also avoid artificial sweeteners because the body was made to function off of *natural* products,–*not artificial* products or sweeteners such as *aspartame*. So beware of eating too much sugar, or of using artificial sweeteners, such as aspartame.

- Avoid any products that contain aspartame. If you do a Google word search of the word "aspartame" and do a little research, you will be shocked to discover how artificial sweeteners such as aspartame, which is found in diet sodas and many other products dangerously affects the body and the brain. If a product says "sugar free" it probably has aspartame in it. So beware! In my research at various websites such as dorway.com At this website, I discovered that "aspartame causes headaches and dizziness, when it reaches any temperature over 86 degrees Fahrenheit, the wood alcohol in aspartame converts into formaldehyde and then to formic acid which is the poison found in the sting of fire ants, and remember formaldehyde is used to embalm people. Furthermore, aspartame does not cause "weight loss" but instead causes weight gain because the heavy metal poisoning from aspartame poisons your metabolism, blocking the burning of calories."

Also, if you read the book *"Aspartame Disease: An Ignored Epidemic"* by Dr. H. J. Roberts you will discover that "thousands of consumers have reported health problems as a result of aspartame."

- Please avoid using *(msg)-monosodium glutamate*, and products or seasonings that contain msg, which is another food additive that has also been reported by many studies to be very harmful. I also recommend that when you grocery shop, do yourself a favor and get in the habit of reading labels. You only get one body, so take care of it and become knowledgeable and wise about what you are putting into **" your body which is the _temple_ of God"** (I Corinthians 3: 16, 17).

We need to control our appetite, and not let it control us? What we do not overcome will overcome us. It's important that we remember that our bodies belong to God and that we were bought with a price, which is the precious blood of Jesus Christ. Therefore, we should not just be putting anything into our bodies.

Some people do not understand that even what we eat and drink is a spiritual matter. I Corinthians 10:31 says: **"Whatsoever ye eat, or drink, or whatsoever ye do, do all to the Glory of God."** So, even our appetite is a spiritual and not just a physical matter. God has health laws in His Holy Word that we need to follow.

- Another thing you can do to take care of your body is to avoid junk foods because they contain empty calories. They lack enough nutritional value to sustain the body, and this is why the body starts to crave for food again not long after eating junk foods because they are high on calories, but short on nutrition. Also, the reason they are called junk food is because they don't belong in your body-temple of God.

- Feed your body with well nourished, fresh foods such as fruits and veggies which are low on calories, but high on nutrition.

- Avoid processed and refined foods that have been processed using chemicals.

- Make sure you get some B vitamins into your diet because a deficiency in B vitamins such as folic acid, and B12 can trigger depression. Citrus fruits, leafy green vegetables, and beans are healthy foods. Bananas, spinach, and brown rice are also rich in nutrients and can boost your mood. They also have magnesium and folate which can decrease anxiety, and improve sleep. Chromium picolinate reduces carbohydrate cravings, boosts energy, and eases mood swings.

- Avoid drinks with any caffeine because the caffeine can negatively affect your mood, as well as be addictive. Instead, drink decaffeinated beverages. Also avoid drinking liquor which can negatively affect your mood because liquor is a depressant.

- Eat nuts like almonds and walnuts, flax, soybeans, and tofu because that way you will be getting your Omega 3's, which play an important role in stabilizing the mood.

- Don't overeat. In Proverbs 23:2, we are told **"And put a knife to your throat if you are a man given to appetite (overeating).** Overeating is responsible for many degenerative diseases. The laws of health are to be obeyed. It is important that the digestive organs shall not be overtaxed. There are some people, who keep the stomach continually at work, and it has hardly any chance to rest, or to maintain its strength and the end result is having digestive disorders.

- Drink plenty of water, especially if you are a smoker to flush some of the nicotine from your system. Instead of drinking drinks which contain caffeine and sugar, which affects the nervous system and can affect your mood, instead drink coffee, or healthy natural herbal teas, and juices which do not contain the harmful, addictive drug caffeine. Also, if you are on medication, caffeine can weaken the effects of your medication.

- Avoid drinking sodas because they have 12 to 16 teaspoons of sugar in them. Technically sugar is not a food, but sugar is actually listed to be a drug, according to the Food and Drug Administration. Therefore, if you drink coffee which has caffeine and sodas which also contain caffeine and sugar, these drinks can wreak havoc on your nervous system. Sadly, many are sickly because of their addiction to coffee, tea, and caffeinated soft drinks.

- Be temperate in all things. **"Everyone who competes for the prize is temperate in all things"** (1 Corinthians 9:25). It is important to understand that true temperance is not eating mostly good things, and just eating a few bad things. *True temperance is eating only what is good for the body, and avoiding everything that is harmful.*

I like to drink juices by Naked. I know that's a strange name for a juice drink, but they taste delicious, and more importantly, they are healthy for you. I think they're called Naked because the drink's ingredients are all natural and fresh. Minute Maid also makes a variety of healthy and delicious juices that you can drink. You can find these juices at Walmart's, and other grocery stores such as Kroger and Ingles, in the juice section.

A neighbor of mine came to my house one night and asked me to help her. She was taking medication, but it wasn't working properly. She was having trouble sleeping; having mood swings, and feeling nervous. I asked her did she drink coffee and sodas regularly. And she told me that yes, she did. So I suggested that if she stopped drinking them, she would probably be able to sleep better at night. You see, caffeine is a stimulant that gives a dangerous artificial boost to the body. Anyway, sure enough, about a week later, my neighbor told me that once she eliminated the coffee and sodas from her diet, she began to feel better, and to sleep better.

- I avoid foods that can negatively affect my brain and mood such as processed sugar, caffeine, alcohol, saturated fats, and foods that have high levels of chemical preservatives such as processed foods. I especially avoid processed foods, refined sugars because they usually have chemicals in them which can be harmful to my body.

- Make sure that with every meal you eat some *live* food. Live food means foods that are fresh and have not been cooked. Our bodies are like a machine and in order to function well, our bodies run off of live foods better than dead, cooked foods. Some people, all they eat is dead food which is cooked food. When we cook our food we lose some of the important vitamins, nutrients, and enzymes that the body needs. So with every meal, try to have some live uncooked food in the form of some fresh fruit, or fresh vegetable salad.

- Instead of frying your food, bake or boil it because it's healthier than frying.

- According to Leviticus 3:17, Gods Word tells us **"This shall be a perpetual statute...you shall eat neither fat nor blood."** Scientific studies have confirmed that most heart attacks are a result from a high cholesterol level in the blood, and the use of fats is largely responsible for this high level of fat in the blood.

- Avoid high-fat dairy products such as cheese, butter, lard and margarine. The best oils to use are extra virgin olive oil, or grape seed oil in cooking. Make your own salad dressings with lemon juice, sea salt, tomato sauce, and extra virgin olive oil. Also, soy cheeses are better for the body than regular, high-fat dairy cheeses.
I used to get cysts and tumors until I started to make wiser food choices, and I switched to a non-dairy, high fiber, and vegetarian diet.

Please carefully consider these vital quotes:

Why the victory over an indulged appetite is so important? "As our first parents lost Eden through the indulgence of appetite, our only hope of regaining Eden is through the *firm denial of appetite* and passion...Thousands of Christians will be lost because they have allowed perverted appetite to overcome them, when IF they had conquered on this point, they would have had moral power to gain the victory over every other temptation of satan." (*Counsels on Diet and Foods, p. 163,* by author Ellen G. White)

"Adam fell by the indulgence of appetite; Christ overcame by the denial of appetite. And our only hope of regaining Eden is through firm self-control." (*Ibid., p. 167*)

Thanks to God and His power, He can help us to overcome fully and completely every craving and desire of an overindulgent appetite. Yes "**I can do all things through Christ which strengtheneth me.**" Philippians 4:13. And so can you.

Dear Beloved, Reader, those are some very important statements, and it would be wise for us to take this matter of our appetites to heart, and ask God to help us to surrender our appetites to Him, so that He can give us the victory over wrong eating habits, and over any indulgence of our appetites.

- Make sure that you get sufficient rest and sleep. Sleep is vital to having a healthy and balanced mind and body. Lack of sleep can cause negative thinking, negative emotions, nervousness, restlessness, and depression. Even too much sleep can cause you to feel depressed and tired. Try to get at least 7 to 8 hours of sleep each night. Develop a regular sleep routine and try to go to bed and get up at the same time every day. And do not exercise at least 4 hours prior to going to bed.

- Make sure that you get exercise. Exercise can make a difference in the way you feel about yourself, and in your general wellbeing. Exercise relieves you of tension because the heart and other muscles are strengthened when they work harder. When you exercise, your *bones become stronger,* your blood pressure goes down, and your mood goes up.

Studies show that regular exercise can be as effective as antidepressant medication at decreasing feelings of fatigue. Exercise releases a natural anti-depressant chemical in the brain and can help you feel like doing something active.

The key to sustaining good mood benefits is to exercise regularly. When you start your exercise routine start small with a simple walk around the block. Then gradually work up to a walking regimen that best fits your needs or comfort zone.

A very good way to exercise is to take walks. If you do not like to walk alone, try to find a walking buddy, or join a regular exercise group, or take your walks on the inside, or the outside of a shopping mall—that way other people will be around you.

While walking, you could also do Music Therapy. Take a small radio, or hand-held CD player and some headphones and listen to classical or Christian music that has an upbeat tempo to it, because if the music has an upbeat tempo, it will lift your spirits and help you to feel upbeat and energized as well.

Dr. Neil Nedley uses Music therapy which has proven extremely successful. Dr. Nedly has helped hundreds of his patients to overcome depression by using music therapy and other therapies. He also has a great book on depression that I highly recommend. For more information, you can check out his website at: Dr. Neil Nedly.com

I exercise by taking *"prayer walks"* to commune with God in nature. This has not only been therapeutic to help me overcome depression, but it has also helped me to have a much closer relationship with God, and has improved my spiritual life.

During my walks, I take time to stop and smell the roses, to appreciate the different bird species, and to feel the warmth of the sun on my face. Then I lift up my voice in prayer to thank God for His beautiful gift of nature.

- On the days that you do not feel like walking, you should still do your best to get some sunshine.

- To take care of your body and to stay in shape you could also participate in some kind of sport. Playing sports is a great way to get regular exercise. And some studies have found that people who participate in sports have fewer symptoms of depression.

- Every day try to get at least 15 minutes of outdoor sunshine. Either walk, or sit and do deep breathing exercises to relax your mind and muscles. Spending time outdoors is very good for the mind and body.

2. Avoid stressful situations which can trigger bouts of depression. Do not overtax your body or your nerves. Learn to manage stress. Set limits on what you're able to do, and adopt healthy eating and lifestyle habits.

3. Keep a daily *Journal* because this can also be therapeutic, and can help you to work your way through fear or depression. Write about your good, or bad experiences, and what lessons you have learned in life from them. Write about your present fears, frustrations, joys, hopes, accomplishments, goals for the future, and how you plan to implement those plans and fulfill them. Write about your happier memories. *You are in control of what you think about.* So make the *choice* to focus on the happy thoughts and the happier memories of your life.

Each day write in your journal about your journey through life. Daily, try to write at least three or more things that are positive about yourself, and about your life's experiences, and accomplishments.

Write about some of the things that bring you joy. Write down how the positive or negative experiences of your life affected you, and what positive lessons you learned from them.

4. Each day in your journal write what I call my: Things to Be Thankful for List. Write your own list. Each day try to write down at least three or more things that you are thankful for, and each day try to add more things to your list until within a 60 day period of time, your list has at least 100 things or more listed on it for which you are thankful for.

For instance, if you were able to get out of bed, that's something to be thankful for, so you could write that down on your thankful list. If it is a bright and sunshiny day outside, you could write down that you are thankful for the sunshine, and thankful to be alive to see it.

You could write about your 3 most favorite memories, and what those experiences felt like. Making a Thankful List is good because practicing gratitude is a habit that will increase your joy and improve your attitude towards your life. Therefore, if you feel depressed you can refer back to your list to remind you of the many blessings you have had to feel thankful for.

5. Control your thoughts. The mind should not be allowed to run rampant. If you're having evil and wrong thoughts, reject them. Say "Stop"! If a negative script keeps re-playing itself in your mind, reject it and erase it. Change the channel of your mind instead to a positive thought, or a positive image.

I remember when I left an abusive relationship, and ended up in a shelter for battered women, I used to visualize an image of seeing my abuser as a big monster. However, the imagination is a wonderful gift that God has given us. So I used my imagination to shrink my enemy down to the size of an ant. Then I visualized throwing the image of him into a garbage can and locking him inside of it so that he could not come out and hurt me anymore. After I did this, the scary thoughts of him stopped haunting me. When I took the giant image that I had of my abuser and shrunk him down to the size of an ant, this helped me, and I overcame my fears of him.

When your mind begins to imagine evil thoughts, immediately turn your focus aside to something positive. Change the channel of your mind from the negative or scary thought to a channel with a positive thought or a positive image. Philippians 4:8 states: **"...Whatsoever things are true, whatsoever things are honest, whatsoever things are just, whatsoever things are lovely, whatsoever things are of a good report; if there be any virtue, or if there be any praise, think on these things."** Therefore, if you are not thinking about things that are lovely, etc., then you should not waste your time thinking about such things.

2 Corinthians 10:3-5 declares **"For though we walk in the flesh, we do not war**

after the flesh. For the weapons of our warfare are not carnal, but mighty through God to the pulling down of strong holds...Casting down vain imaginations and every high thing that exalteth itself against the knowledge of God, and bringing into captivity every thought to the obedience of Christ." *You can bring every wrong thought into captivity or bondage by rejecting it; by throwing it out of your mind.* As soon as a bad thought comes to your mind, don't entertain it, don't dwell on it, but *immediately reject it and cast it down to the ground. Or c*ast it *out* of your mind because the thought may not be coming from you, but from the devil trying to put his evil thoughts into your mind.

Having an evil thought is not sin. It only becomes sin if you desire it, or lust after it, or dwell on it. If necessary, pray and ask God to take the evil thought away. Ask Him to take away your old, carnal, fleshly mind and give you a new, *spiritual mind,* which is the mind of Christ. Philippians 2:5 says, **"Let this mind be in you, which was also in Christ Jesus."** However, notice that we have to surrender and *"let or allow"* Jesus' mind to abide in us. Once we have the mind of Christ, we will not have a mind filled with depression, because the mind of Christ is not depressed.

When a wrong thought comes to your mind, you can say aloud, "I take that thought captive and I rebuke it by the mighty Name of Jesus Christ," or "I bind that evil thought and plead the blood of Jesus Christ over my mind." When evil thoughts come, they are thoughts that are raised up against God; therefore, we have a duty to *cast them down*, or to cast them *out*.

We will have many mental struggles until we recognize and reject the thoughts that the devil injects into our minds. I will talk about how to control the thoughts in greater detail in a later chapter.

6. Spend time each day reading the Holy Bible, and this can help to overcome depression or fear. Instead of spending time on Facebook, put your face into God's holy book.

I get so much joy from studying God's Word. At first, reading the Bible may seem boring, or difficult, but the more you read it, the more you will understand it and enjoy it. And eventually reading the Bible will become one of the most enjoyable parts of your life.

The book of Psalms is filled with many wonderful, inspirational verses that are sure to lift your spirits. There are many motivational true stories in the Bible, such as the story about Daniel in the lion's den, the story about how God used Moses to deliver the Israelites from their Egyptian enemies, the story of Joseph, and so many more great Bible stories that will encourage you and strengthen your faith.

Also, in the Bible God reveals His will for our lives. Some people are depressed because they don't know the divine purpose and plan that God has for their existence.

7. Another way to overcome depression is to remove yourself from the company of angry people, or people who are always talking negativity and discouragement. Avoid people who bring your mood down. If you surround yourself with negative people who like to complain, or argue, or gossip, or find fault, or cause strife then you will find yourself having some of those same characteristics. Being around people who are negative can negatively affect your mood and cause depression. Don't let people steal your joy, or your peace of mind. Instead, *choose* to be around people who can increase your joy and peace, and help you to have a positive outlook on life.

8. Intentionally think positive thoughts instead of negative thoughts. Thoughts have energy, and if your thoughts are negative, you will attract negative experiences to you. So try to *practice* having positive thoughts about your life and future. What are you doing in your mind? Maybe you need to do some housecleaning in your mind and sweep

out those old dusty negative thoughts, and retrain your mind to dwell on positive thoughts.

One way to have positive thoughts is by avoiding watching soap-operas, or worldly television programs, because they are filled with negative story-lines about stealing, murder, adultery, lust, dishonesty, vice, and violence. If you partake in watching other people's problems, or other people's sins, it will bring you down emotionally. Also avoid watching any movies that convey negative messages, immorality, or scenes of violence. The question we should ask is: *"Would Jesus watch this?"* And if the answer is no, then we should not watch it. Garbage into the mind will produce garbage coming out in the form of negative thoughts and emotions.

9. Do something fun and creative like taking photographs, drawing or painting some pictures, get a new game to play, do some arts and crafts, go to the beach, go swimming, take a picnic, take a drive, or ride across the country side to enjoy the view, travel to a place you've never traveled to before, play with your child or pet, do a Word-Find puzzle, or Cross-word puzzle, or put together a Jigsaw puzzle.

10. Be optimistic. Some people only look at the negative or discouraging details of life, instead of focusing on the positive things that happen to them. Have a positive attitude towards your future. Just because bad things have happened to you, does not determine what will or can happen to you today or in the future. Plan for the best, and expect the best!

11. Read Inspirational Poetry by poets such as Helen Steiner-Rice, or read poetry from my poetry book called, *Good News in a Bad News World*. If you enjoy inspirational poetry, my poetry book is filled with many uplifting and motivational poems!

If you ever feel like giving up, please try to remember the encouraging words to this poem that I wrote.

DON'T GIVE UP!

Don't give up no matter what you do.
Don't give up, God will see you through.
Sure the blow was hard when it hit.
But still you must not quit.
Don't Give Up!
Don't dwell on how bad things seem.
Don't you know that God can redeem?
Don't Give Up!

Things are not as bad as they could be.
They will get better just wait and see.
Don't Give Up!
Things may appear to be hopeless,
But looks can be deceiving.
You just keep on trying and believing.
Don't Give Up!
Many have failed to reach the top.
But they kept trying and did not stop.
Don't Give Up!
You may not have a job or any money.
But God can make your life prosperous and
Sunny.
If You Don't Give Up!
Your goal is not impossible to achieve.
Faith, courage, and persistence are all you need.
Don't Give Up!
It will be a great day for you,
When you see your hopes and dreams come true.
Don't Give Up!
**DON'T YOU DARE, DON'T YOU DARE -
GIVE UP!**

12. Let go of the past. Letting go of your past regrets allows you to make powerful decisions in your present life. Allow yourself to be free from those things that hurt you and have contributed to you being depressed or fearful. You don't have to forget the past, but you must forgive those who have hurt you in the past if you ever want to experience freedom and true peace of mind.

If someone has hurt you, try to forget about them. You cannot change them, nor can you change the past. However, you can change your future. Only you can determine that you will learn from the mistakes, the bad relationships, and the hurtful experiences of your past so that you will not repeat them again.

Instead of beating yourself up and dwelling on your past hurts or mistakes, ask yourself what have you learned, and what will you do differently so you won't repeat making the same mistake again.

It is a waste of valuable time if you are constantly thinking about your enemies, or about someone who has hurt you deeply. *Stop letting your enemies win by dwelling on them? Stop allowing the pain that they caused you to win, and to take up your precious time. Do not keep giving them honor by reliving in your mind what they did to hurt you. Let it go. Let them go. Bury thoughts of them in the cemetery of your imaginary mind, and set yourself free right now!*

Allow yourself to be released from your past tragedies, and start living for today and making positive plans for your tomorrows. Stop honoring your pain, stop honoring your abusers by thinking about them, and reliving what they did to you. Instead start looking forward to the many blessings and joyous experiences that await you. *Stop letting the pain win, and start letting the healing begin!*

Don't give thoughts about your enemies one more thought, because while you're dwelling on them, they are going on with their life. Therefore, you need to go on with your life. Also, don't keep talking about the past. Talking about the past only causes you to keep reliving the bad experience. *Stop looking back because you're missing the blessings waiting in front of you!*

13. *Get your mind off of yourself* by volunteering, or by doing good deeds to help others. If you visit a hospital, you won't be focused on your own problems as you turn your attention to see people there who are much worse off than you are. Live to be a blessing to this world. Let your life be an instrument of God's love, then consequently, more blessings and more love will come back to you.

Whenever the opportunity presents itself, use your life to *do good and kindly deeds for others.* It will make you feel happy to be a modern-day Good Samaritan. By performing simple daily acts of kindness, this contains a "double blessing" for you, the giver, and for the receiver of your kind deed. This is the Law of Reciprocity, which means that as you give, it comes back to you; whether you give good deeds or evil deeds. As Luke 6:38 gives this promise: **"Give and it shall be given unto you; good**

measure, pressed down, and shaken together, and running over, shall men give into our bosom. For with the same measure that ye mete withal it shall be measured to you again."

If possible, give to the less fortunate. Being generous and giving can actually increase your own joy. Instead of money and material possessions having power over you, giving them away gives you power over money and material goods. And as you give joy to others, joy will return to you!

Some people are depressed because they dwell on themselves too much. When the mind dwells upon self, or on our enemies, it is turned away from God, who is our Source of peace, joy, and life. It is satan's constant effort to keep our attention diverted from God, our Creator, and instead on the pleasures of the world, our problems, our sorrows, the faults of others, or on our own faults. Thus, by separating us from focusing on God, and His goodness, the devil hopes to gain the power over our minds.

14. Train yourself to talk positive; to talk hope and faith. Watch the words that you speak. Use your mouth to bless yourself instead of cursing yourself. The tongue is a powerful tool we can use for good or evil. **"The power of life and death is in the tongue"** Proverbs 18:21. Your tongue and your words that you speak can

either be a great asset to you, or be an enemy. So what are you claiming with your mouth and with the words you speak? Blessings or cursings?

Instead of saying, "I am cursed." Say "I am blessed." Instead of saying, "I am worried." Say "I believe! I am trusting God to help me get through this." Instead of saying "I am sick." Say, "I believe that I will get well."

What are you speaking over your life, your health, and your future? If you've had the habit to speak negative, retrain yourself to speak positive words over your life. It takes time to overcome bad habits, but you can do it!

Let go of disempowering language, like "Oh, I'm such a loser." Just because your circumstances are unpleasant does not make you a loser. You are not what you are based on your circumstances, because your circumstances can change in an instant. You are what you are based on your thoughts of who you perceive yourself to be. Remember what the Word of God tells us: **"As a man thinketh in his heart so is he"** Proverbs 23:7.

If you begin taking the necessary steps to improve your circumstances, then they will change. Just the mere fact that you are alive makes you a winner. Having money and possessions does not make you a winner. Just by virtue of you being a one-of-a-kind created being by God makes you valuable and uniquely special.

The Holy Bible tells us that: **"You will have what you say."** So remember to always speak life, speak health, speak blessings, speak prosperity, speak faith, speak hope, speak joy, and speak peace over your life.

15. Do not complain, but train yourself to have the *attitude of gratitude*. God hates it when we complain. As bad as things may be, they could be a whole lot worse. Also, why complain about things that you cannot change? It's hard to feel depressed when you're focusing on your blessings. Therefore, focus on the positive blessings in your life.

When someone asks you how you are feeling, instead of trying to find something sad to tell them to gain their sympathy, instead say, "Oh, I am doing great. Life is so good, and it's going to get even better!" Let your conversation be cheerful. If you choose to focus on the positive things in your life, this will help you to have joy and peace. There was one particular time that I felt so glum and deeply depressed, but I just started singing an uplifting hymn, and before I knew it, I had sung my way into joy and rejoicing!

Please ponder the important words to this poem. I sincerely pray that the *good news* in this poem will encourage and inspire you to be thankful in all things, and to never complain.

STOP COMPLAINING!

We have so much to be thankful for.
So let's not complain like we did before.
If it's raining, don't complain.
It's better to have rain rather than a hurricane.
If it's snowing, don't complain.
It's better to have snow rather than a tornado.
If it's hot and one hundred degrees,
It's better than having a blizzard freeze.
If it's cloudy today, it may be sunshine
Tomorrow;
So stop your complaining and sorrow.
Today you may not have any money.
Tomorrow you might have plenty.
Complaining is wasted energy.
So instead count your blessings.
Life and circumstances are constantly changing.
So stop complaining.
Why complain and whine?
Instead try to have positive things on your mind.
The pain you're feeling today;
Tomorrow it may be all gone away.
If life seems all gloom and doom,
Trust it will get much better soon.
Instead of complaining, Praise the Lord!
Your thankfulness will make Him want
To bless you even more!

16. Some people are depressed because they have resentment in their hearts. Forgive yourself and forgive those who have hurt you. *Forgiveness is a necessary step towards spiritual growth, and emotional peace.* We must be willing to forgive, because the Holy Scriptures of God tells us that if we do not forgive, then God will not forgive us. (Matthew 6:14). Forgiveness may not be easy, but it is necessary.

First, you must forgive yourself for thinking that you are perfect and that you would never make mistakes. You need to forgive yourself if you trusted someone that you should not have trusted. You need to forgive so that you can have the ability to trust again, but this time learn the lesson not to trust people until they first earn your trust and have proven themselves to be trust-worthy.

It takes courage and integrity to say "I'm sorry." Maybe you are depressed because you need to confess some sin to God, and repent and turn away from that sin. Perhaps you are depressed because you are holding onto resentment and you need to forgive, or you need to make things right with someone that you yourself have wronged, and you need to ask for forgiveness. Today set yourself free through forgiving yourself, or forgiving anyone who has hurt you deeply, or by asking God to forgive you, or by asking the person whom you hurt for forgiveness.

17. Do things to feed your soul. Meditate on the goodness of God, pray, get a massage, take a warm bath, listen to some soothing music, pick some flowers, or take a picnic at a beautiful park.

18. Make some popcorn and watch some funny comedies to make you laugh such as: I Love Lucy TV program re-runs, Home for Christmas, or Steve Martin's comedy, The Jerk. Laughter is very therapeutic, and has a power to heal. **"A merry heart does good like a medicine"** Proverbs 17:22.

We all need to laugh more. If you want to laugh more, make the *choice* to do it. If you want to be happy, *choose* to be happy!

19. If you feel depressed or lonely, join a social group. At one time I was very

lonely, so I joined a writer's group. I really enjoyed getting to meet other writers and share my writings, and hear the writings of other writers. There are many groups that you can join. Go online and Google the words: social groups, or meet-ups.com, or poetry groups, and so on.

Also, to keep from being lonely you could go to the park, or to the shopping mall and sit while you watch people go by. It can be entertaining to look at how some people look funny or interesting as they pass through the park or malls. And if someone comes and sits next to you, perhaps you can strike up a conversation with them. Remember, **"He who makes friends, must show himself to be friendly"** Proverbs 18:24.

20. Take a weekend vacation just to get away to relax, or have some fun. When I lived in a suburb in Georgia, I went to downtown Atlanta, Georgia. I checked myself into a nice hotel room and just spent the weekend sight-seeing and enjoying myself. You don't have to leave the country to take a vacation. You can take a get-away trip even in the state that you reside in. It's inexpensive, and can still be very enjoyable.

21. Learn to be *content*. Some people are depressed because they are never satisfied. However, money or things don't bring any real lasting satisfaction. Happiness is not only a feeling, but it is a state of mind. *Choose* to be happy, cheerful, and content with what you have. We are not the sum of how much money we have, or of the possessions we have accumulated. Life is more important than money or things. Unfortunately, some people get their self-worth from money, or their possessions. However, this is a superficial view of life.

You are priceless whether you have a million dollars in the bank, or whether you have no money in the bank. You are very precious, and you have value whether you live in a mansion, or in a tent. Jesus Christ said, "**Foxes have holes and birds have nest, but the Son of man has not anywhere but to lay his head.**" So, even though Jesus was God, and the Messiah, yet, basically, even He was homeless.

22. Do little things to show appreciation and love for yourself. *Pamper yourself* by getting your hair done, or styled in a different way than the norm, or by getting

your nails done, or buy yourself some flowers, or fix your favorite soup for lunch. Little things that you do out of love for yourself can really help to bring joy to your heart, and lift your spirits.

23. Studies have shown that St. John's Wort has been a very helpful herb to help people overcome the symptoms of depression.

24. Write a letter to yourself telling yourself about the positive things that you like about yourself, and about how much you appreciate the good things you have accomplished in your life. Try to use many positive comments about your life as a special and unique gift to the world from God. Make sure that this letter is at least one page long, and do not say one negative thing about yourself in the letter.

25. Do not try to please everybody, because you can't. Don't be a yes man or yes woman every time someone asks you to do something for them. If you try to please everybody else you'll make yourself unhappy. Learn to say no and mean it. No is not a bad word, however, it helps to set boundaries and limitations. It helps to protect you from people abusing you, or taking you for granted. You teach

people how to treat you. Therefore, if they treat you badly, it may be because you have allowed it. So, stop allowing it. You don't have to be mean, but you don't have to allow it either.

26. Do "*Self–talk.*" Talk yourself through your depression, or fear, or guilt, or worry. If you talk faith, you will have faith. If you talk sickness, you will have sickness. Speak positive affirmations. *Affirmations* and the words you speak have power. Affirmations are the power to bring about occurrences into your life by your speech.

Affirmations are words that declare and proclaim a situation to be true. What do you want to be true about you or your life? Affirmations are bringing forth to life energy in a positive or negative way into the universe. God spoke this world into existence, He said **"Let there be light"** Genesis 1:3, and there was light.
An affirmation can be positive or negative. You are creating your destiny with the words that you speak. You can bless or curse your life by your words. The words that you speak on a daily basis are determining your life experience, and your future.

Examples of Affirmations are: "I have value and worth, and my life has purpose." "I am willing to change my life by learning how to love myself." "I will have positive, happy, and fulfilling relationships with people because I am a positive and happy person, and I am living a happy and fulfilling life." "I am not afraid, because God has promised that He has not given me the spirit of fear, but of power, and of love, and of a sound mind." "A merry heart does good like a medicine, and I am happy and healthy, because I have a merry and cheerful heart."

27. Finish this sentence: "I would feel better if only I…" Or this one: "I would be happy if…" Then think about the things you could do to make this desire become a reality.

28. Make *determined efforts* to have happy experiences, and fulfilling relationships for your future. For example, if you desire to get married, this won't happen if you just stay at home and don't socialize to meet your potential mate.

29. Do not fear rejection. Rejection does not mean you have failed. It just means you need to go in another direction and do

something else, or you need to try another method to reach your goal. Failure is giving up, or letting fear prevent you from trying again to succeed.

30. Smile. Every day give your smile away to the people you see on a daily basis, then, a smile will come back to you from someone else. A cheerful smile to others will bring joy to your own heart. Put a smile on our face, or force yourself to laugh. What you put out to the universe comes back to you. I have noticed that when I'm in a good mood and smiling it seems more people are actually smiling back at me. I look at a smile as giving someone a gift that they didn't have to pay for, and that does not cost me a thing to give it. A smile is one of the simplest ways of showing God's love and compassion to your fellow human being. A smile will build your confidence and the confidence of those who you give a smile to. A smile is like a boomerang. As you send it out to others, their smiles will rebound back to you.

31. Another thing you can do to overcome depression is to: Make a list of at least five activities that motivates you emotionally and that lifts your spirits.

Then try to fit at least one of them into your regular, weekly schedule.

32. Attend a local lecture or seminar on topics that might improve your life, and uplift your spirits.

33. Do not read or watch anything on TV that conveys violence, or a negative message. Whatever you take in through your eyes and ears, either feeds your spirit or drains your spirit. Some people feed themselves physically, yet starve themselves spiritually due to the negative movies, negative music, and negative books that they feast their eyes and ears on.

34. Memorize some of the precious *promises of God* in the Holy Bible, and claim them for your life, especially when you're not feeling well; speak those promises to your body, to your mind, and to your life!

35. Watch by yourself, or invite some friends or family members over to watch some movies with positive motivational messages such as the wonderful Christian movies: War Room, Facing the Giants, Flywheel, Fireproof, Courageous, God Is Not Dead, or the remake of The Ten Commandments.

36. Write a letter to someone who has hurt you severely. Tell them how you feel, read it out loud, and then tell them that you forgive them, then, throw the letter away, and if negative thoughts come back to you about how they hurt you, remind yourself that you have forgiven them and you have moved on in your life and left that experience buried in the past.

37. Get a pet so you will have something to take care of, and not have to be centered on just yourself as much.

38. Some people are depressed due to having been rejected. Don't let obstacles or rejections cause you to feel depressed, or stop you from moving forward, but rather let them push you through to achieving your goals.

I have experienced a lot of rejection in my life. However, I have discovered that the times I was rejected, was the times that God had something much better in store for me to have. Rejection or obstacles do not mean that you are a failure. They just may mean that you need to turn and go another direction, or try another method to achieve your desired goal.

39. Find a quiet place in your home or somewhere else where you can spend at least 30 minutes to an hour having some quiet "me-time." Tune out the noises and distractions around you. And tune into hearing the still, small voice of the Creator speaking to your heart. And do not let the phone, or anything, or anyone distract you during this private time. If you do not take care of yourself you cannot take care of your family. Some people are depressed because they never get any private, quiet time.

40. Once a week, invite a good friend out to lunch, or over for lunch. Then, in your conversation with them talk *only* about positive subjects of discussion.

41. If you are facing a problem, instead of dwelling on it, take about fifteen to thirty minutes thinking about how you can move from the problem into a solution. Nothing will change or improve unless you put forth the energy and effort to change it, or improve it.

42. Attend community events, festivals, Christian conventions, or Christian music concerts. Be sociable and try to establish some new friendships with your fellow neighbors.

43. Some people need to confess their sins and forsake them, because sometimes having sin in our lives can cause us to be depressed or fearful. Also, if we have sin in our lives this can give the devil the right to harass our minds' with depression and with fear.

It is quite often the case that many times people have depression and fear, and they do not realize it is because they are under attack, and evil spiritual forces are at work. If you are experiencing panic attacks, depression, or fear then it may be necessary for you to do some spiritual warfare. However, don't attempt to fight the devil and his demons alone. Pray and ask God to help you. Perhaps you have sinned, or done something that has given the devil rights to torment you with depression or fear, and you need to simply repent and ask God to take His authority over you and your mind.

First, we need to understand some of the ways that satan can gain access to our minds, and how he uses this access to control a person's mind.

In an article written by Pastor John Grosboll entitled: *How the Devil Gains Access to Your Mind, "In His Steps," newsletter,* the March 2010 edition, he gives many of the different ways the enemy of salvation can gain access to our mind. It is mostly by our own allowance.

"There are many different ways through which the devil can gain access to our mind:

"By Spiritualism and getting involved with the occult, psychics, or the zodiac, Through an unconverted spouse, By sinning or sinful indulgence, Wrong music, By forbidden marriages or associations, By idleness, By cheap conversation, By the study of false science, By other human beings who are children of disobedience, By careless indifference towards God, By disobeying parents to be free from restraint, By not making a complete surrender to Jesus as our Lord, By making of none effect the Holy Bible and not obeying Bible teachings, By perverted appetite, By yielding to the thoughts that the devil suggests."

I have just given you a brief list here, but if you want a copy of the complete article which goes into more details about each point, just send me an email and I'll send it to you via through the mail. So leave your mailing address.

Fear and panic attacks…

Panic attacks are becoming a real problem these days. The devil tries to use fear to keep Christians in bondage. However, fear is just one of the devil's weapons.

What are some of satan's other weapons?

satan's weapons come in the form of doubt, depression, discouragement, fear, anxiety attacks, family strife, mental torment, deception, guilt, feelings of hopelessness, hatred, prejudice, envy, jealousy, lusts, temptation, and so on. satan tries to hold us captive through our thoughts, feelings and emotions.

The Battle for the Mind is Real

Unless we *choose* to indulge in the devil's temptations he cannot control us. Thus, who controls the mind depends upon the choice made by the individual. Therefore, everything depends on the right action of the will...and the *will* is our *power of choice or decision.* God gives us the "free will" to choose to do right or wrong. And either our *will* (power of choice and decision) is on the Lord's side, or it's on the devil's side.

How Do We Invite Christ's Control?

We can invite Christ to control us by *yielding to Him in obedience.* Every morning and night I rededicate my life, my mind and body to God. If you have never given your will to God, but you want to, then tell the devil you are taking your will from him and giving it to God. Then tell God that you are giving your will to Him.

"When we give our will to Christ, He does not take it away from us or destroys it. He purifies it and gives it back to us to use in service for Him... Our will is to be yielded to Him, that we may receive it again, purified, and refined, and so linked in sympathy with the divine that He can pour through us the tides of His love and power." (*Thoughts from the Mount of Blessings, MB, p. 62)*

"God has placed in the mind of each accountable person the power to exert his own will. While it is true that either one power or the other has control of one's mind, yet, until we have sinned away our day of grace, we are free to exert our own will, to exercise our own free choice. We need not continue to accept the influences and suggestions of satan, or to be controlled by him. Persons who are under the influence or control of the evil spirits break with satan, and be converted so that they may be controlled by the Holy Spirit of truth.

"We must choose Christ to be our master; otherwise if we reject Christ and continue to live in sin, we are choosing satan to be our master. Give your will to God so that He can work and will in you to do of His good pleasure. But we must give our will to God. God accepts nothing less than absolute surrender of the mind, heart, the will, the strength, the entire being, to His control… Daily you must learn the meaning of self surrender." *(Manuscript Release 64, 1904)*

"Philippians 2: 13 states: **"For it is God which worketh in you both to will and to do of His good pleasure."** The whole heart must be yielded to God, or the change of the new birth experience can never be wrought in us by which we are to be restored to His likeness. Pure religion has to do with the will. The will is the governing power in the nature of man, bringing all the other faculties under its sway.... The will is the deciding power which works in the children of men unto obedience to God or unto disobedience." (*Faith I Live By, p 152*)

We Must Choose Decidedly

"Our surrender must not only be full and complete, but also positive. We can choose satan as our leader inadvertently by yielding to him, merely by failing to decidedly choose Christ. It is not necessary for us deliberately to choose the service of the kingdom of darkness in order to come under its dominion. We have only to neglect to ally ourselves with the kingdom of light. *If we do not cooperate with the heavenly agencies, satan will take possession of the heart, and will make it his abiding place. The only defense against evil is the indwelling of Christ in the heart through faith in His righteousness."* (*Desire of Ages, DA, p. 324*)

If we do not wish to be controlled by satan, we must knowingly and consciously surrender to Christ, because those who are not purposefully followers of Christ are servants of satan either willingly, or by neglecting to yield themselves to be under the control of God. **"His servants ye are to whom ye (yield yourselves) to obey"** (Romans 6:16).

As I stated earlier, some people are depressed or fearful because they are under attack by the powers of darkness. Here are some things that you can do to combat evil forces when you are in the battle of spiritual warfare. Also, here are some of the *spiritual weapons* you can use to defeat the forces of darkness:

- Call on Jesus and His Holy Spirit to fight your spiritual battles for you. The devil and his demon hosts tremble at the sound of Jesus' name. When the devil is trying to put evil thoughts into your mind, rebuke and bind those evil thoughts by saying, "In the name of Jesus Christ, I rebuke and bind that thought and cast it down." Or say, "Heavenly Father, please appropriate the merits of the blood of Jesus Christ over my mind, over my thoughts, and over my body."

The devil hates it when we praise Jesus' Name, and there's power in His holy Name!

Consider the words to this poem about the Mighty Power in Jesus' Name!

JESUS NAME!

JESUS! The name above every other
Name.
JESUS! The name we can always claim.
JESUS! The name above earth and
Heaven.
JESUS! The name we can call on 24/7.
JESUS! The name that can calm a raging
Sea.
JESUS! The name that can save you and
Me.
JESUS! The name that is full of awesome
Power!
JESUS! The name that is beautiful like a
Flower.
JESUS! The name that causes devils to
Tremble and fear.
JESUS! The name that I love to hear.
JESUS! The name to call on when feeling
Stressed.
JESUS! The name to cry out to when
Facing death.
JESUS! The name of the one who
Supplies our needs.
JESUS! The one who died on Calvary to
Set us free!
JESUS! The name that protects us from
Danger and calamities.
JESUS! The name that shields us from
Our enemies.

JESUS! The name we can call on when
Confused.
JESUS! The name we can depend on
When alone and friends are few.
JESUS! The name of the one who loves
Us so.
JESUS! The name of the one we must
Never let go.
J-E-S-U-S!
And you never have to guess;
You know it's the wonderful name of
Jesus.
But JESUS is much more than just
Another Name.
**It is a force more powerful than a
HURRICANE!**

- One of the very powerful *spiritual weapons* that you can use when you are depressed, fearful, or under attack by the forces of darkness, is to *quote or read sacred Bible Scriptures*, when possible this should be done *out loud*. The devil and his evil demons hate to hear the Bible being read out loud.

- Singing good, sacred, Christian songs is also another wonderful and powerful *spiritual weapon* that can drive demons away. "Redeemed", "Jesus Loves Me", and "How Great Thou Art" are good ones that you can sing.

- As I mentioned, earlier, please avoid putting anything into your mind that is evil, such as watching movies, or reading books that contain immoral acts and violence. Especially *avoid soap-operas,* which are filled with immoral acts, dishonest deeds, and acts of violence. Instead, fill your mind with spiritual, uplifting, pure, and heavenly things. Listen to Christian music instead of secular music, which many times conveys messages of immorality and vice.

- When you're depressed, or under spiritual warfare attack, *intentionally focus your mind on the goodness and power of God, and on His blessings,* instead of on any wrong thoughts, or problems.

- *Praise* is another powerful *spiritual weapon* we can use to overcome depression, or fear. Sometimes when I have felt depressed, or afraid, or feelings of guilt, I began to *praise* God in order to get my mind off of myself, or off of my problems.

Praising God is a great spiritual *weapon* we can use when under attack by the powers of darkness. I remember, one day the devil was really attacking my mind. The devil was trying to put me on a guilt-trip about things that I had done a long time ago in my past.

I felt so depressed, but I also felt impressed to just start praising God, and the more I praised Him; the more things I thought of to praise Him for. I just started thanking God for His awesome goodness, and for all of His blessings. You might want to try this. You can thank Him *out loud*, and, or you can get a sheet of paper and start writing down the things you have to be thankful to God for.

You will be surprised how this can help you begin to feel happier and better. Surely you can think of something to be thankful for. Thank God for your life, for your body, for the air He's given us to breathe, for the trees, for the flowers, or for the beautiful blue sky. Just keep writing things down, and before you know it you might have a full page, or several pages of things to thank God for.

I also should mention that if you suspect someone that you meet, or that you have met to be a possible evil agent of satan, avoid any physical contact with that individual. Do not take anything from them, because it will cause you to establish a "soul-tie" with them. If you have taken anything from them, get rid of it, in order to break and renounce any un-godly soul-tie with them.

I talk more about this and the issue of spiritual warfare in greater detail in my book: *Defeat the Powers of Darkness with Spiritual*

Warfare. In that book, I explain how to know when you are under attack by the powers of darkness, how to recognize if a person is demon-possessed, how to use Jesus' method to cast out demon spirits, plus the book includes spiritual warfare prayers.

Sadly, many dear people run to an exorcist's, or to a deliverance ministry when they are dealing with spiritual warfare, but really what they need to do is learn what the "spiritual weapons" are that God has given us, and how to use them effectively to defeat the powers of darkness.

44. Another crucial thing you can do to overcome depression is to *pray,* and then pray some more! *Prayer* is also another essential and powerful *spiritual weapon* you can use to overcome fear, depression, and the powers of darkness.

Pray fervently and ask God to help you overcome depression, fear, guilt, worry, and the powers of darkness. There have been times when I was feeling almost overwhelmed with depression and fear. Consequently, I knelt down on my knees and petitioned God to help me. When dealing with problems, instead of sending someone an *email* asking them for help, we need to get on our knees and send God a *knee-mail* and take our problems to the Lord in prayer because He is the Great problem Solver! So I prayed fervently and diligently. And as a result, God in

His infinite love and mercy took away my sadness, and vanquished my fear. The Holy Bible declares: **"God is able to do exceedingly, abundantly, above, anything we ask or think."** I have seen this Bible verse fulfilled in my own life, so I know that this promise of God is true. In fact, all of God's precious Bible promises are true. However, in order to receive His help, you have to first ask in faith, not wavering in doubt or unbelief.

At first, when you pray, it may seem difficult. Your mind may tend to wander. However, if your mind wanders, bring it back to your prayer. And ask God to help you stay focused. Also, if you remain diligent, your prayer life will become a joy and a stabilizing force in your life that will produce great results; not only for your life, but for the lives of those you pray for.

- "The darkness of the evil one (satan) encloses those who neglect to pray. The whispered temptations of the enemy entice them to sin; and it is all because they do not make use of the privileges that God has given them in the divine appointment of prayer. Why should the sons and daughters of God be reluctant to pray, when prayer is the key in the hand of faith to unlock heaven's storehouse, where are treasured the boundless resources of Omnipotence?

"Without unceasing prayer and diligent watching we are in danger of growing careless and of deviating from the right path. The adversary seeks continually to obstruct the way to the mercy seat, that we may not by earnest supplication and faith obtain grace and power to resist temptation." (*Messages to Young people, MYP, p. 96)*

- "Satan trembles at the sound of prayer. Satan dreads prayer by the humblest saint." (*Prayer, p.270)*

Prayer Is the Key That Can Set Us Free!

I cannot emphasize enough the importance of *prayer*! Many dear people are depressed or fearful due to a poor or complacent prayer life.

The most important thing that helped me to be able to overcome fear, guilt, depression, worry, restlessness, nervousness, making dumb mistakes and wrong moves, illnesses, and defeating the powers of darkness, was through *fervent and diligent prayer!*

Prayer is the Key and the Solution to life's problems and issues!

There has been countless times when I felt discouraged, or lonely, or a sense of hopelessness. But after I knelt down to pray, it wasn't long before I felt lifted up in my spirit and I could feel a sense of happiness spring up in my heart. I felt as if God was holding me in His loving arms. Some times when you are feeling sad you may not feel like praying, but that is the time when you should pray most of all.

If you want to have happiness and peace in your heart, spend quality time sitting at the feet of Jesus—seeking the Lord in prayer, and it will give you strength for the day, as well as cause your sadness to disappear. James 5:16 tells us: **"The effectual fervent prayers of a righteous man availeth much."** Hebrews 11:6 says: **"God is a rewarder of them that *diligently* seek Him."**

- *"Prayer is the opening of the heart to God as to a friend... Prayer does not bring God down to us, but brings us up to Him."(Steps to Christ, p. 93)*

Prayer is a mighty weapon that we can use against satan. Therefore, Beloved Reader, please *do not neglect prayer*!

- **"Prayer breaks the snare of satan.** When we feel the least inclined to commune with Jesus, let us pray the most. By so doing we shall break satan's snare, the clouds of darkness will disappear, and we shall realize the sweet presence of

Jesus."(*SDA Bible Commentary, vol. 2, p. 1008*)

If we allow the devil to cause us to neglect prayer and the studying of the Holy Scriptures, we will most assuredly be overcome by his attacks. Therefore, the devil has invented all kinds of inventions to engross our minds; to distract us from establishing an intimate relationship with God, our Creator.

What has the devil invented to distract you from prayer? Is it television?, or the cell phone?, or Ipads, and Ipods?, or the computer? or your job?, or material possessions?, or money?, or your car?, or worldly ambition?

It would be very beneficial to you emotionally and spiritually to get into the routine of having morning and evening devotion. During my devotions, I sing hymns of praise to God, and I pray and study the Holy Bible. We can complain about our problems until we are blue in the face. But the key and the solution to solve those problems, is for us to *pray!*

Thoughtfully consider the important words to this next poem. I hope and pray that the words bless you.

MUCH PRAYER MEANS MUCH POWER!

Pray in the morning, at noon, and at night.
Prayer is a weapon we must use to win the fight.
Through prayer you will find,
Peace for your troubled mind.
God bows down to listen when we bow down to
Pray.
God is interested in the words that we say.
When burdens have you backed against a wall.
Prayer will help you not to fall.
Prayer helps us to grow in grace.
Prayer will lift you up when you've fallen on
Your face.
If you want the devil to flee and run away,
Just get down on your knees and pray.
If you want to defeat your enemies,
Just get down on your knees.
Sometimes it may seem like God is not listening.
But it's just a test to see if you will pray without
Ceasing.
Prayer is the universal language that God loves to
Hear.
Our prayers are like music to His holy ears.
Never think that prayer is just a waste of time.
Prayer is the most important thing you can do
With your mouth and mind.
Pray when you have money and when you have
None.
Pray through all your trials until the victory is
Won.

Pray for yourself, your family, and your friends
Too.
Even pray for your enemies who hurt and trouble
You.
So pray always, and even in the midnight hour.
Because **MUCH PRAYER MEANS MUCH
POWER!**

If you want to overcome depression and fear
then you must not neglect to pray and ask God to
help you. *The closer we draw to God in fervent
prayer, the further the devil moves away from us.*

> **45.** Make sure that you have been *born again
> and converted.* I think this is the *most
> important* thing you can do to overcome
> depression, fear, or any emotional, or
> physical illness. Therefore, I saved this
> vital point for last. Some people are
> depressed, fearful, or feeling guilty due to
> sin in their lives, and because they are not
> in a right relationship with God.

When we have died to self and to our old,
carnal, fleshly sin nature, and have the new birth
experience, we should not be depressed, or
fearful, or feel guilt.
The Christian life is not a life of sadness,
sorrow, or fear, but a life of joy and peace of
mind in Jesus Christ, as we allow Him to abide
and dwell in us moment-by-moment each day. In
John 10:10 it states that **"He (Jesus) came that**

we might have life, and *life more abundantly.*"
There is joy in the Lord! **And "The joy of the
Lord is our strength"**, says the Bible. There is
hope, and faith, and freedom in the Lord; not
depression, fear, worry, guilt, or bondage.

Personally, I have discovered that
depression and fear and guilt can stem from sin.
When we have sin in our lives, **"sin separates us
from God,"** according to Isaiah 59:2.

Another shocking thing that I discovered
from God's Word is that our (*sins can actually
cause good things to be withheld from us*), as it
states in Jeremiah 5:25, **"Your iniquities (sins)
have turned away these things, and your sins
have withholden good things from you."** Wow!
Just, think, if we have sin in our lives, we could
actually be cutting off our own blessings from us.
How tragic!

Furthermore, when we sin, it gives satan
certain rights to us; to harass or torment us.
Whether we want to admit it or not when we
have sin in our lives we are what the Bible refers
to as the **"children of disobedience"**, (Ephesians
2:2), or satan's children, and this gives him more
access to his children of disobedience. However,
his access to God's children; the **"children of
obedience"**, is limited and hindered because they
are protected by God and covered under the
protective blood of Jesus Christ. This is why it is
critical that we get sin out of our lives, and we
plead the merits of the blood of Jesus Christ over

our minds, over our bodies, over our family members, and over our homes and property.

"Fallen man is satan's lawful captive. The mission of Christ was to rescue man from the power of his great adversary. Man is naturally inclined to follow satan's suggestions, and he cannot successfully resist so terrible a foe unless Christ, the mighty Conqueror, dwells in him, guiding his desires, and giving him strength. God alone can limit the power of satan."(*Testimonies to the Church, vol. 1, p.341*)

We must learn how to exercise our *wills* properly. We must learn to put and keep our wills on the Lord's side, and allow His will to be done in our lives instead of our own wills.

"But you must remember that your *will* is the spring of all your actions. (*Much depends on the right action of the will.*) *Your will is your power of choice and decision.* This *will*, that forms so important a factor in the character of man, was at the fall (of Adam and Eve) given into the control of satan; and he has ever since been working in man to will and to do of his own pleasure, but to the utter ruin and misery of man. But the infinite sacrifice of God in giving Jesus, His beloved Son, to become a sacrifice for sin, enables Him to say, without violating one principle of His government: 'Yield yourself up to Me; give Me that will; take it from the control of satan, and I will take possession of it; then I can work in you to will and to do of My good pleasure!" (*Testimonies to the Church, vol. 5, p. 515, italics supplied*)

While, it is true that some people who have depression may have a chemical imbalance in the brain, however, I contend that a great many of the mental illnesses that a lot of people are dealing with are a result of *sin*. Their depression or mental illness stems from something that is wrong *spiritually* in their lives. If only they would repent and turn away from their sins and turn completely and unreservedly to God, then He would heal their mental as well as their emotional health and well-being.

If some people would just become truly born again and converted, then the devil and his demonic spirit's harassments, power, control, influence, and manipulation upon their minds and bodies would be broken.

Somehow, when I was coping with depression, and my emotional and spiritual warfare issues, I knew in order for satan's power over my mind to be broken, I had to give my heart fully to God, put away my sins, and become a new creature in Christ through having the "*new birth*" experience, and then I would receive the *spiritual mind of Christ,* which does not have any depression at all.

In the Holy Bible, it is written, **"Let this *mind* be in you which was also in Christ Jesus"** Philippians 2:15. If we are given the *spiritual mind* of Christ, then we won't have depression because the mind of Christ does not have depression. But notice it says: "let". We have to let Jesus give us His mind. We have to be willing to humble ourselves and let go of trusting in our own limited wisdom, and submit ourselves to relying on the unlimited wisdom of Christ.

After I became born again and converted, and Jesus gave me a new heart, which means a new *spiritual mind,* then my symptoms of depression, fear, guilt, and worry went away. When Jesus began to live in me through the person of His Holy Spirit; and I received the mind of Christ, I became calm, and my mind was at peace because I had given Jesus my old, carnal, fleshly mind which was full of depression and anxiety. In exchange, He gave me a new *spiritual* mind— His mind which is full of peace, joy, hope, faith, restfulness, courage and happiness. I'll talk more about the benefits of the *new birth* experience later.

Chapter
2

The Way You Can Overcome
Fear and Guilt

How to Get Rid of Fear

Instead of being afraid, have faith and trust in God. Some people are depressed or afraid because they have not learned to trust Jesus, and to look to Him and live. They have not learned to put their hope and confidence in Almighty God, but have put their trust in feeble human beings, or in their own selves.

Jesus promised, **"I will never leave you nor forsake you"** Hebrews 13:5. Take Jesus at His word. Believe His promise. Only the sense of God's presence can drive away the fear that the devil tries to bring to our minds. Claim this promise from Psalm 34: 7 which states, **"The angel of the Lord encamps round about them that fear Him, and delivers them."**

- The best way to get the devil to leave you alone is to speak the Word. Therefore, memorize and quote Scriptures *out loud* that will enforce your faith and build you up instead of tear you down. Train yourself to operate out of the mind of Christ, then, you will find His thoughts filled with cheerfulness and praise, versus complaining, being critical, or negative, or doubting, or being fearful.

Memorize God's precious promises, and say them *out loud* when feeling fearful. Memorize Scriptures that will give you hope, and joy, and faith, and peace! The Word of God is like a Mighty Sword and it can quench the fiery darts of the enemy. The devil hates it when we throw the truth of the Word of God in his face.

Please carefully consider the following:

- Stop being fearful; how can you have fear and faith at the same time? Fear drives faith away. Some people are fearful of events that will never take place, or depressed about things that have occurred so far back in their past, yet they continue to resurrect those old negative memories, instead of burying them.

- When the devil uses fear to tell you that you can't, or tries to convince you that you are hopeless, or stupid, or ugly, or that you are not good enough, or that you are a bad person, do not listen. The devil wants to use fear to bring you down and to convince you that you will be hurt, or disappointed, or rejected, but fear is a liar, and the devil is a liar. The devil is a bully who tries to use fear, guilt, shame, despair, and doubt to cause us to give up.

- Stop listening to the devils lies and deceptions. I invite you to be the *happy* and *courageous* person God created you to be; and to accomplish the things you desire to achieve. Tell fear to get lost and go bury itself in a cemetery where it belongs. Refuse to let fear hold you back. Go forth and do what you need to do, and be what you need to be, and say what you need to say, and think the positive thoughts of hope and faith that you need to think. Also, ask God and He will help you, because the Holy Bible says: **"You have not because you ask not."**

- Fear reveals unbelief, but faith takes God at His word. In order to not be fearful, you need to get your mind off of others, or off of yourself, and look up to Jesus! God cares for everything and everyone whom He has created. No tears are shed without Him noticing. If we would believe this, then despair would not overtake us, and all our worries would vanish.

- Have faith in God! Faith is to trust God in all of life's experiences, good or bad.

Many people trust God when things are going good, but not when things are falling apart. They do not have genuine faith. If we have real faith, we would know unconditionally that God has our best interest at heart.

• Don't make the mistake of accepting the devils thoughts as your own. If fear is coming to your mind, then this fear is not coming from God, because God does not give us a spirit of fear. God gives us a spirit of faith; a spirit of hope; a spirit of peace; a spirit of joy! Believe God's Word instead of believing the devil's lies that he's been injecting into your mind.

• When fear comes, or when evil thoughts come, an evil spirit is often behind the fear, or behind the evil thoughts. So pray, "Dear Heavenly Father, please rebuke and bind the devil, or the evil spirit that is bringing that evil thought to my mind." The Bible says to **"cast down imaginations."** Therefore, do your duty and bind and cast those evil thoughts or evil images down. You may have to cast evil thoughts down repeatedly.

• I'm constantly filling my mind with right thinking on positive things; or on spiritual and heavenly things—on God's goodness, and on God's wonderful promises. I don't have time to entertain negative thoughts. Keep wrong thoughts out of your mind by keeping your mind full of right thoughts. Use your mind for the purpose it was made for; such as to Praise God! Keep your mind on praising God. We are told: **"Thou will keep thee in perfect peace whose mind is stayed on Thee"** Isaiah 26:3. God will keep our minds in perfect peace IF we keep our minds on Him and on spiritual things. Keep thoughts of the Lord and His awesome goodness ever before you. I only listen to sermon messages and sacred Christian music, because I want to keep my mind stayed on the Lord. I sincerely pray that the words to this next poem will help to increase your faith, and bring a warm sense of joy, confidence, and peace to your mind!

YOU MUST HAVE FAITH!

When things look bad,
And you're feeling sad,
You must have faith.
When you're confused,
And don't know what to do;
You must have faith.

When bills are due,
And your dollars are few;
You must have faith.
When your car is running on empty,
And you have no gas money;
You must have faith.
When you don't have a job and you're out of
Work,
And your family and friends are acting
Like unconcerned jerks;
You must have faith.
When you feel like you just can't cope,
And you're running out of hope;
You must have faith.
When it seems God is not listening,
Or you think He has stopped caring;
You must have faith.
You must trust God no matter how
Discouraging things look to you.
Because things can turn around unexpectedly
Very soon.
You must have faith even when you don't
Feel like believing.
Just hold on because a mighty blessing
You will be receiving.
Then all of your long suffering will be
A thing of the past,
And you will be able to rejoice at last,
Because you KEPT THE FAITH!

Having faith is very important to overcoming depression and fear.

What Is Faith?

Many people have fear because they lack having faith and trust in God.

- "Faith and feeling should not be confounded together. They are distinct as the east is from the west. In the darkest hours is it then we should exercise faith, and not suffer our feelings to govern us, but press our faith through the dark clouds to the throne of God and claim the blessing of Heaven." (*5 Manuscript Releases, p. 231*)

- "Not because we see or feel that God hears us are we to believe. We are to trust in His promises. When we come to Him in faith, every petition enters the heart of God. When we have asked for His blessing, we should believe that we receive it, and thank Him that we have received it. Then we are to go about our duties, assured that the blessing will be realized when we need it most." (*Desire of Ages, DA, p. 200*)

How to Get Rid of Guilt!

- "Give your feelings of guilt to the Savior. Jesus Speaks Pardon! Satan seeks to draw our minds away from the mighty Helper, to lead us to ponder over our degeneration of soul. But though Jesus sees the guilt of the past, He speaks pardon; and we should not dishonor Him by doubting His love." (*Testimonies to the Church, vol. 1, pp. 345, 346*)

The devil loves to make people feel guilty. First he lures us with the temptation to sin then if we fall into temptation and commit the sinful act; he tries to make us feel overwhelmed with guilt. However, with God's help we can overcome any feelings of guilt.

Don't wallow in feelings of guilt. Instead ask God for forgiveness and believe He has forgiven you. In 1 John 1:9 we are promised: **If we confess our sins, He is faithful and just to forgive us our sins and to cleanse us from all unrighteousness.**

- "This feeling of guiltiness must be laid at the foot of the Cross of Calvary…Now Jesus says, Lay it on me; I will take your sin, I will give you peace. Destroy no longer self-respect, for I have bought you with the price of my own blood. You are Mine; your weakened will I will strengthen; your remorse for sin, I will remove. Then turn your grateful heart…and lay hold on the hope set before you. God accepts your broken, contrite heart. He offers you freedom and pardon. He offers to adopt you into His family, with His grace to help your weakness, and the dear Jesus will lead you on step by step if you will only put your hand in His and let Him guide you." (*Mind, Character, and Personality*, vol.2, p. 452, 522, 1977)

If you have sinned and asked God for forgiveness, believe He has forgiven you. Therefore, who are you not to forgive yourself? Forgive yourself, pick yourself up, and go forward pressing on in faith and peace of mind.

Chapter
3

The Way to Control Your Thoughts

In order to experience happiness, you need to guard your thoughts. If you are focusing your mind on negative things, it will manifest itself in you having a thinking pattern of thinking negative thoughts.

"As a man thinks in his heart, so is he" (Proverbs 23:7). We must guard our thoughts, because thoughts can become actions. Actually thoughts become habits and habits become actions and actions become a person's character. God wants to help us bring **"every thought into captivity to the obedience of Christ"** (2 Corinthians 10:5). Cast those evil thoughts down to the ground. However, satan desperately wants to bring negative and evil thoughts into our mind. When the wrong kinds of thoughts come to your mind, don't entertain them for a second because many times these thoughts did not originate from you, but the devil is trying to put them into your mind. But immediately close the door of your mind and reject them.

How to Control Your Thoughts?

"For though we walk in the flesh, we do not war after the flesh: (For the weapons of our warfare are not carnal, but mighty through God to the pulling down of strong holds) Casting down imaginations and every high thing that exalteth itself against the knowledge of God, and bringing into captivity every thought to the obedience of Christ" 2 Corinthians 10: 3-5.

When we have wrong thoughts what does it mean to **"cast down vain imaginations, and ...bring into captivity every thought to the obedience of Christ?"** We take an evil thought captive by exercising Christ's authority over it (Mark 16: 17-18, Luke 10: 19-20.) And in the name of Jesus binding that evil thought.

We cast down wrong thoughts by rejecting them. This is "binding" the evil thought. And ask Jesus to rebuke and bind the evil spirit that may be bringing evil thoughts to your mind. When an evil thought comes to your mind, stop it! Use the Sword of the Spirit, which according to Ephesians 6:17 is the spoken Word of God. Therefore, speak the Word of God to that thought. For example, if a thought of fear comes, say, 1Timothy 1:7, **"God has not given us (me) the spirit of fear, but of power, and of love, and of a sound mind."**

Sometimes the devil tries to put strongholds into our minds by putting wrong thoughts into our minds.

What is a Stronghold?

A stronghold is a false belief in a lie of the devil, which is contrary to the Word of God, controlling our decisions and personal activities in life. A stronghold is holding onto a sin or habit instead of allowing God to give us the victory over it, as He has the power to do. Such as: *unforgiveness* can become a stronghold, because God tells us to forgive one another.

Consider these final points on overcoming fear, guilt, depression, and *wrong thinking*.

- When you make a decision to change your mind, and your wrong way of thinking, the thoughts of depression, fear, and guilt should go away.

- Romans 12:2 states: **And be not conformed to this world: but be ye transformed by the *renewing* of your mind, that ye may prove what is that good and acceptable, and perfect, will of God.**" I want you to especially notice the words **"be ye transformed by the *renewing of your mind.*"**

How can you have a *renewing* of your mind?

Simply by stop thinking negative thoughts and by having new ideals, new and positive thoughts; the mind is *renewed*. Therefore, change your thoughts. Just because the devil offers evil thoughts, does not mean you have to accept them. If he offered you a deadly disease would you accept it? No! You would immediately repel his offer. Likewise, reject his evil thoughts. Purposely activate your mind and line it up with God's Word and God's will.

- Instead of accepting the devil's thoughts of fear, or guilt, or whatever; intentionally choose positive thoughts to dwell on from God's Word. As long as you think that the devil's evil thoughts are your own thoughts, you will never experience victory. When you change your thinking, your life will begin to change.

- Set your mind on things above, not on things on the earth. Have you ever meditated on what it will be like to live in Heaven? Sometimes, I have sat and contemplated just how I am going to build my home in Heaven. After all, the Bible states that we will be able to "build houses." Let your mind ponder about Heaven, and how you will build your heavenly home and furnish it. Keep your mind on good things. Start choosing right thoughts. If you have been born again, you should have received a new heart (new mind), so why are you thinking the same old bad thoughts of your old carnal mind?

- Think according to the mind of Christ. What will His thoughts be like? They will be positive. Jesus was a cheerful person. Everywhere He went His words were uplifting and positive. Train your mind to have positive thoughts and positive expectations. Don't engage in negative conversations, but positive ones. You are not operating with the mind of Christ by thinking negative thoughts. Sadly, many suffer from depression, fear and guilt due to negative thoughts.

- Keep your mind on God and not on the problem. Some people have fear because they are trusting in their own feeble strength to correct the problem, instead of trusting in God's Omnipotent power. When we do not ask God for help, this is a form of pride. Some people are "me-focused," and they focus on themselves. Or some people are "they-focused". They focus on their enemies, or they focus on others to help them. And some people are "problem-focused," but instead we need to be "God-focused." Jesus said, **"I am the way, the truth, and the life."** The solution is having an intimate relationship with Christ, and trusting Him to handle our problems, and our enemies for us.

- Understand that God loves you! Meditate on His love for you, and you will experience it. You need to become consciously aware of God's love for you and confess it out loud. Confess it and say it. "God loves me." If you really knew how much God loves you, you would not be afraid or depressed. You need to feel confident in His love and know that He can take you through the most difficult trials. The only thing that can limit Him is your lack of faith. However, you do have some faith; otherwise, the devil would not be trying to steal your faith away from you. The Holy Bible tells us that we are **"all given a measure of faith."** It is what we do with that faith that counts. And we need to practice *exercising* our faith, then, our faith will grow.

"There is no fear in love; but perfect love casteth out all fear" I John 4: 18. God loves you perfectly just the way you are. Ask Him to help you to love Him perfectly by obeying Him in every aspect of your life. And when you have that perfect love and trust in God, you will not be fearful, because by having that abiding, love relationship with God, this will cast out all fear away from you!

Ask God to reveal to you if you are willfully, or ignorantly disobeying Him in any area of your life, and if that area of disobedience is preventing you from having perfect love for Him, or preventing you from having happiness or peace of mind.

Are you operating out of the mind of Christ? If so, you will not be thinking about how bad you are. Have Christ–based thoughts, which are about who you are "in Christ." And "in Christ", you are loved. If God did not love you He would not have sent His Son, Jesus to die for you on the Cross, and to pay the penalty for your sins.

When we dwell on our bad faults, or on the faults of others, we drive God away. Jesus said **"If I be lifted up from the earth, I will draw all men unto me" Job 12:32.** Lift Jesus up by thinking positive thoughts that are in line with His Word. Lift Jesus up through prayer; through Bible study, and through praising Him, then He will draw you closer to Him, and lift you up in your spirits!

- Do not waste precious time living under guilt, fear and condemnation, thereby living under the will of the devil. Instead, live under the will of God, which is thinking good thoughts about knowing that **Jesus "came that we might have life, and that we might have life more abundantly"** John 10:10.

- Every time a negative, condemning thought comes to your mind; remind yourself by saying out loud that God loves you. Say, "I am not afraid, but I am trusting in God's love." "I am improving and changing for the better," "I am growing spiritually." "God has a wonderful plan for my life." These are the *truths* you must think on instead of thinking on the false thoughts of the devil telling you his lies.

  I will say it again: *Choose* to be happy, and *choose* to think positive thoughts. This is what you are supposed to be doing with your mind. Think deliberately according to the Word of God. Don't receive the devil's thoughts as your own thoughts. Ignore the devil and begin thinking right and uplifting thoughts.

- Make a *rule* of your thoughts: If it's bad, don't think about it, or say it. If it's good, then think about it and if necessary, say it.

- Praise God in your words and thoughts. Whenever you hear something positive, get in the habit of saying, "Praise the Lord!" Determine to be joyful no matter what your circumstances are. Have the attitude of Psalm 34:1, "**I will bless the Lord at all times; His praises shall continually be in my mouth.**" We can bless the Lord by letting His praises be continually in our thoughts and in our mouths.

- Be a grateful person. A grateful person does not have time to be depressed, or afraid because they are too busy focusing on the things to appreciate and be thankful for. Some people are so focused on themselves until they miss the blessings all around them.

- Thoughts and words have a healing or destructive power. Are you using your thoughts and words to glorify God and bring healing to yourself? Or are you glorifying the devil and helping him to destroy you by thinking his evil thoughts, and speaking his negative words that he has been influencing you to think and speak?

- Line up your thoughts with the Word of God. You are not walking according to

God's Word if your thoughts are opposite to what it says. For instance, if your thoughts are of fear, the Word says: **"God has NOT given us the spirit of Fear."** So if you have fear, your thoughts are not lining up with the Word of God. Fear certainly never makes anything better, so why not give it back to the devil because that is where the spirit of fear came from?

If you are worried, this thought of worry does not line up with God's word, which teaches us not to worry. The Word of God declares to us in Matthew 6: 34, **"Be anxious (or do not worry) for nothing."** Therefore, what are you worrying about? God's Word says that we are to **"Trust in the Lord, and lean not unto thine own understanding."** Therefore, you need to obey this instruction from God's Holy Word.

I want to share with you a story from Joyce Meyer's book: *Battlefield of the Mind*: It is a story about a man who was dealing with spiritual warfare due to the lies of the devil.
Fear is an attack from satan upon the mind. Your mind was created to be at rest and at peace. So use your mind for the purpose it was created; to be at rest, and at peace, and to have trust in God.
There was a man who was sick and who was confessing the Word over his body, quoting healing Scriptures and believing for his healing

to manifest. While doing so, he was intermittently attacked with thoughts of doubt.

After he had gone though a hard time and was beginning to get discouraged. God opened his eyes to the spirit world. This is what he saw: a demon speaking lies to him, telling him that he was not going to get healed and that confessing the Word was not going to work. But he also saw that each time he confessed the Word, light would come out of his mouth like a sword, and the demon would cower and fall backward.

As God showed him this vision, the man then understood it was so important to keep speaking the Word. He saw that he did have faith, which is why the demon was attacking him with doubt...

Fear is not something God puts in us. The Bible says that **"God gives every man a ...measure of faith"** (Romans 12:3). God has placed faith in our heart, but the devil tries to negate our faith by attacking us with doubt.

Doubts come in the form of thoughts, and are in opposition to the Word of God. This is why it is so important for us to know the Word of God. If we know the Word, then we can recognize when the devil is lying to us. Be assured that he lies to us in order to steal what Jesus purchased for us through His death and resurrection." *(p. 105)*

The next time you feel stressed, or depressed, or afraid or worried try to remember the important, comforting words to this next poem…

DON'T WORRY – GOD IS IN CONTROL!

Some people don't believe that God exist.
They think He's nothing more than a fairy tale or
Myth.
They say in order to believe
They need something they can see or feel;
Then they would know that God is real.
But the evidence of His existence is all
Around us.
In His creation of nature it is obvious.
God is more real than human eyes
Can see.
God is just as real as you and me.
And God is in control of everything!
When you're confused and don't know
Which way you should be going;
Ask God. He knows the end from the
Beginning.
If you lose everything you've
Been living for.
God can replace it with so much more.
If your life begins to fall apart;
God can put it back together as fast as a beat of
Your heart.
If your enemies outnumber you by fifty;
With God on your side the two of you
Are the majority.

If the doctor gives you a bad report,
And says your life will be cut short;
It's not over until God says it's over.
You can be healed and recover.
If the devil attacks you like a raging flood.
God can turn it around for
Your good.
If your spouse says they're leaving you
For another.
God can give you someone better.
When it seems the whole world is
Against you.
And your family and friends have
Failed you to;
God promises 'I will never leave you
Nor forsake you.
If I be for you who can be against you!'
So don't worry! GOD IS IN CONTROL!

Dear Beloved Reader, Jesus speaks to you: **"Peace I leave you..."** John 14:27. Accept His offer of peace and reject the devil's offer of fear.

Instead of being afraid, trust God. 2 Corinthians 5: 7 declares, **"For we walk by faith, not by sight."**

Faith is not a feeling; it is taking God at His Word and trusting in Him unconditionally. Romans 10:17, **"So then faith comes by hearing, and hearing by the word of God."** Consequently, if you want your faith to grow, saturate your mind by listening to spiritual things such as Christian sermons, and Christian music. The devil will try to convince you not to do this, but do not listen to him. Ask God to help you not to listen to the devil, and to help you not to think the devil's thoughts, but to think God-centered thoughts, and to listen to God's voice.

Philippians 4: 8 states: **"Whatsoever things are true, honest, just, pure, lovely, and of a good report, if there be any virtue, or if there be any praise think on these things."** If the thoughts that invade your mind are not on things that are lovely, or pure, or of a good report, then don't think about them, but cast them away from your mind.

In order to have positive thoughts you need to feed your mind with positive things, otherwise garbage into the mind will produce garbage out of the mind. What things are you feeding into your mind? And what are your eyes beholding throughout the day?

Carefully consider the following quotes from the *Amazing Facts Publishing, Study Guide 26*:

Your choice of TV programs and all of your conduct should be guided by the Word of God and not by your own feelings.
Christians must separate themselves from all things that are not true, honest, just, pure, lovely, and of a good report. They will avoid:

A. Dishonesty of every kind-cheating, lying, stealing, being unfair, intent to deceive, slander, and betrayal.

B. Impurity of every kind. This includes fornication, adultery, incest, homosexuality, perversion of all types, pornography, profanity, filthy conversation, dirty jokes, degenerate songs, or music, and most of what is shown on television and in movie theaters.

C. Places where we would never invite Jesus to accompany us, such as nightclubs, taverns, gambling casinos, racetracks, etcetera.

Many types of secular music (rap, country, pop, rock, heavy metal, adult contemporary, and dance music) have been largely captured by satan. The lyrics often glorify vice and destroy a desire for spiritual matters.

The question that we should ask ourselves when we choose music or movies is, "Would such music or movies please Jesus?" And if the answer is no, then we should avoid them.

God has provided for His people plenty of good music that inspires, refreshes, elevates, and strengthens the Christian experience. Those who accept the devil's degrading music as a substitute are missing one of life's choicest blessings. Remember, if Christ can participate in an activity with you, you are safe. If not, stay away from it!

Do the things you watch on television appeal to your lower or to your higher nature? Do they lead you into a greater love for Jesus, or for the world? Do they glorify Jesus, or evil sins and vices? One study said 'that without TV, there would be 10,000 fewer murders per year in the United States, 70,000 fewer rapes, and 700,000 fewer assaults." (*pp. 6, 7*)

If you sit in front of the TV and behold evil, it has a negative influence on the mind and character. If you watch other people sinning on TV, God counts it as you vicariously taking part in their sinful acts. Anything you love more than Jesus can be an idol. If your conscience tells you not to watch something because it is evil and you still keep watching it, you are violating your conscience, and the voice of conscience is the voice of God. Therefore, it is very dangerous to violate conscience. I had to get rid of my TV because it was causing me to sin. I was spending too much time watching TV and neglecting prayer and Bible study. I felt convicted by the Lord to get my TV set out of my house. I'm very happy that I did because watching TV was too much of a temptation.

I actually got rid of my TV because most of the things on it were negative; including the news—it seemed to be all bad news. And besides, I was spending more time in front of the TV than I was spending at the feet of Jesus Christ.

The devil has corrupted and captured the minds of many people through television. Tragically, many professed Christians have been beguiled by TV until the point that they can't even pull themselves away from it. It's as if they are addicted to it like a dangerous drug.

I also got rid of my TV years ago because the Holy Spirit convicted me that if I continued to spend countless hours watching TV and neglecting praying and studying the Bible, then I would end up lost. My TV was like an addiction to me also. I was not watching anything that contained sexual perversion, or profanity, or violence, but I was watching the Home Channel. I thought watching programs about remodeling homes was safe, but it wasn't safe because I was wasting precious hours viewing these programs instead of spending time seeking to establish and maintain a personal relationship with God.

Let's face it— much of what is on TV is not of God. The devil is using many secular songs and TV programs and movies to corrupt the minds and morals of many, including professed Christians. There are programs like Jerry Springer where the guests on the program fight each other like animals. This program is barbaric to say the least, and I know that Jesus, our perfect example, would certainly not watch such programs that encourage the human beings that He created to act like brute beasts. satan laughs at such behavior, but God and holy angels weep when they see God's professed followers watching such inhumane and devilish programs.

I recall years ago, that once I removed the TV set from my own house, all of the arguments between me and my son ceased, and we began to talk and communicate peacefully. But later when I brought the TV back into the house, my son and I started to argue again. I finally got rid of the TV once and for all, and I am so glad that I did. Anything we place before spending time with God can be an idol; even your television set can be an idol if you spend more time watching it than you do with the spiritual, the heavenly, and the eternal things of God.

"By beholding we become changed into the same image" (2 Corinthians 3:18). This means we become like the things that we repeatedly hear or look at with our eyes. Be careful what you listen to, and what you look at with your eyes because these things can seriously hinder your spiritual growth, and negatively affect your thought patterns, and cause you to have wrong thoughts. You can't have peaceful thoughts if you are beholding violence with your eyes. In 1 Thessalonians 5:22 it states: **"Abstain from all appearances of evil."**

What if Jesus returned one day and found you sitting watching something ungodly on TV, do you really think that He would take you to heaven with Him? No, you would be left behind to die with the rest of the wicked. Tragically, it seems many people will be lost due to their wrong choices of watching evil TV programs. You can purchase some really good inspirational music and movies at www.christianbooks.com or www.christianmovies.com.

Chapter
4

The 7 Key Ways to Overcome a Quick Temper

Another way to be happy is by learning to have patience, and to let go of a quick temper that has perhaps been stealing your joy, and your peace. It's been said that "patience is a virtue", and this is true.

There are those who profess to be Christians, yet they are impatient. Revelations 14:12 states: "Here is the **patience** of the saints. **Here are they that keep the commandments of God, and the faith of Jesus.**" We can't be one of God's saints if we do not have the important character trait of patience.

"Christis our example. We are forming characters for heaven. No character can be complete without trial and suffering. We must be tested, we must be tried. Christ bore the test of character in our behalf that we might bear this test in our own behalf through the divine strength He has brought to us. Christ is our example in patience, in forbearance, in meekness and lowliness of mind. He was at variance and at war with the whole ungodly world, yet He did not give way to passion and violence manifested in words and actions, although receiving shameful abuse in return for good works. He was afflicted, He was rejected and despitefully treated, yet He retaliated not. He possessed self-control, dignity, and majesty. He suffered with calmness, and for abuse gave only compassion, pity, and love.

"*Imitate your Redeemer in these things.* Do not get excited when things go wrong. Do not let self arise, and lose your self-control because you fancy things are not as they should be. Because others are wrong is no excuse for you to do wrong. Two wrongs will not make one right. You have victories to gain in order to overcome as Christ overcame. Christ never murmured, never uttered discontent, displeasure, or resentment. He was never disheartened, discouraged, ruffled, or fretted. He was patient, and calm and self-possessed under the most difficult and trying circumstances...He had a calm inward joy, a peace which was serene. His will was ever swallowed up in the will of His Father. Not My will, but Thine be done, was heard from His pale and quivering lips." *(Letter 51a to "Dear Children, Edson and Emma White, Sept. 11, 1874, from Ellen White, italics supplied)*

The lives of some people are without peace and joy because as soon as the slightest problem arises they quickly lose patience and lose their temper. However, having a quick temper, and having impatience accomplishes absolutely nothing except to frustrate themselves and those around them.

Some people are missing out on experiencing the joy, and peace that God intends for them to have because they either lack patience, or they have an unhappy disposition, or a quick temper. I've even heard some people say that they can't control their tempers. But this is not true. You can control your temper. For example: If your boss at work tells you to do something that you don't want to do, do you curse them out and fight them? No. You may get angry but you control your temper because you don't want to lose your job. Ecclesiastes 7:9 tells us: **"Be not quick in your spirit to be angry for anger rest in the bosom of fools.** In other words, having a quick temper is foolish.

"He that is slow to anger is better than the mighty, and he that rules his spirit than he that takes a city" Proverbs 16:32. It is not a strong person who loses his temper, but a weak person. It takes a strong person to keep himself under control, but a weak person quickly loses control of themselves. In Proverbs 25:28 it is written: **"He that has no rule over his own spirit is like a city that is broken down and without walls."** James 1:19 states: **"My beloved brethren, let every man be swift to hear, slow to speak, slow to wrath."**

"Strength of character consists of two things: power of the will and power of self control. He who is mastered by his passions is a weak man. The real greatness and nobility of the man is measured by his power to subdue his feelings and not by the power of his feelings to subdue him or her…

"The strongest man is he who, while sensitive to abuse, will yet restrain passion and forgive his enemies." (*Steps to Christ, SC, p. 84*)

Are you controlling your temper? Or is your temper controlling you?

"Never should we lose control of ourselves. It is a sin to speak impatiently and fretfully. We are to walk worthy giving a right representation of Christ. The speaking of an angry word is like flint striking flint. It at once kindles angry feelings. Never should those who claim to be followers of Christ speak harsh words, but we are to follow Jesus' example. When people mistreated Him, or spoke the wrong way to Him He spoke to them with firmness, but He never lost control of Himself. The highest evidence of nobility in a Christian is self-control. Some have come up without self control…They have not bridled their tongue or their temper and yet they claim to be Christ followers, but they are not. Jesus has given them no such example. Those of us who claim to be Christians must be careful of the words we speak and never lose control of ourselves.

"There are many who have never felt the necessity of subduing self, and overcoming wicked tempers. They cherish bitterness and anger in their hearts and these evil traits of character defile the soul. They thus deny Christ, and darken the pathway of others. None will be excused for the exhibition of uncontrollable tempers. Thousands will miss out on heaven through their want of self-control. When persons profess to be Christians and their religion does not make them better men and better women in all the relations of life – living representatives of Christ in disposition and character –they are none of His." (*Sons and Daughters of God, p. 142)*

"We cannot be fretful and impatient and still be Christians, for a fretful and impatient spirit is not the Spirit of Christ. You cannot indulge your own temper and have your own way and still remain the children of God. We shall have to struggle with our hereditary tendencies that we may not yield to temptation and become angry under provocation. The man who yields to impatience is serving satan. The holy Bible says: **"To whom you yield yourselves servant to obey his servant you are to whom you obey"** Romans 6:16.'" (*Review and Herald 8-14-1888*, italics supplied)

"satan takes the control of every mind that is not decidedly under the control of the Spirit of God. Let no one deceive his own soul in this matter. If you harbor a quick temper, pride, self-esteem, a love for the supremacy, vainglory, unholy ambition, complaining, discontent, bitterness, deception, slandering, gossip, you have not Christ abiding in your heart and the evidence shows that you have the mind and character of satan, not of Jesus Christ who was meek, humble, and lowly of heart." *(Mind, Character, and Personality, vol. 2, p. 522)*

The following quotes come from the book, Mind, Character, and Personality, vol. 2, by author, Ellen G. White.

"Anger opens the heart to satan. Those who at any supposed provocation feel at liberty to indulge anger, or resentment and to loose their temper are opening the heart to satan. Bitterness and animosity must be banished from the soul if we would be in harmony with heaven." I know of one particular instance in which a lady lost her temper so bad until a demon entered her. As a result, she suffered for many years until she was finally born again and when Christ entered her the demon was cast out.

How to overcome having a temper?
1. *When you get irritated, refuse to speak.* Let those who are easily irritated refuse to retaliate when words that anger them are spoken. We should crucify self, in the place of seeking to crucify others. Jesus said: **"If any man come after me, Let him deny himself and take up his cross and follow me"** (Matthew 16:24).
Meet Anger with silence. There is a wonderful power in silence. When you find yourself becoming impatient, when impatient words are spoken to you, do not retaliate. Do not return evil for evil. Words spoken in reply to one who is angry usually acts as a whip lashing the temper

into greater fury. But anger met by silence quickly dies away.

Let the Christian bridle his tongue, firmly resolving not to speak harsh impatient words. With the tongue bridled, he may be victorious in every trial of patience through which he is called to pass.

2. *Cultivate a Kind Conciliatory Spirit.* Let no feeling of retaliation come into your mind. We have but a little time in this world, and let us work for time and for eternity. Be ready to confess your faults and forsake them so that your sins may go beforehand to judgment and be blotted out. An uncontrollable temper can be conquered. The teachings of Christ carried out into the life will elevate man. Those who strive to subdue their natural defects of character cannot be crowned by Jesus unless they strive to overcome by being found often in prayer seeking help from God.

3. *Resist resentful feelings, and don't make excuses for having a temper.* When we make excuses for sin we are cherishing sin. Jesus came to save us from our sins, not in our sins. Confess your angry temper to God and ask God to help you. It doesn't matter if you inherited your temper. God has the power to deliver us from both hereditary and cultivated habits and sins. So do not make excuses and don't blame others if you lose your temper. We cannot change what we do not acknowledge. No one made you lose your temper. You made the choice to lose your

temper and with God's help you can choose to control your temper. (*p. 522)*

4. The next time you are tempted to lose your temper *do not yield to the temptation.* Instead stop and pray and ask God to help you to remain calm. Quickly yield to the Holy Spirit to control your spirit; otherwise the devil will take control. James 4:7 states: **"Submit yourselves unto God, resist the devil and he will flee."** If you submit to God He will control your temper and the devil will flee. But if you submit to the devil then you are resisting God, and the devil will control your temper, and God will flee. You must surrender your spirit to God so that He can control your spirit, otherwise the devil will control your spirit.

5. *Use God's methods* when dealing with problems and with people. God's methods are: love, kindness, patience, self-control, gentleness, meekness, humility, peacefulness, honesty, tolerance, long suffering and forgiveness.

6. *Ask God to help you to not use satan's methods* when dealing with people or with difficult circumstances, which are: impatience, pride, yelling, cursing, seeking revenge, outburst of anger, resentment, deception, strife, dishonesty, bitterness and hatred. It's up to you who you allow to control you and your spirit.

How can we go to heaven having a temper and not having self-control? We would be in heaven going off on people. God cannot let anyone into heaven who does not have a converted character. In Ephesians 5:27 it tells us that **Jesus is coming back for a church "without spot, wrinkle or blemish.** What are spots, wrinkles, and blemishes? They are character defects.

God wants to give us the victory over our sins and defects of character. And He can give us victory if we give them to Him. We must all reflect God's character if we want to live with Him in His holy Kingdom. We were created in God's holy image and with His character traits of love, patience, gentleness, goodness, peaccfulness, and self-control.

7. If you have a problem with your temper, *ask God to help you to develop habits of self-control. Ask God to help you become born again and converted, and to help you to be like Christ.* We need to be willing to accept the attributes of Jesus' character so that we can reflect His character to our fellow man. We must be willing to give God our minds and our wills. Our *will* or the *will is our power of choice and decision.* The *will* is our power to choose or to decide whether we will listen to and obey God, or whether we will listen to and obey the devil. It is our power to choose right or wrong, good or evil. We must give God the right to control us; otherwise the devil will take control.

If you have a temper, pray and ask God to help you to remain calm when you are tempted to lose control of your temper. We all need the abiding presence of God's Holy Spirit within us because it is He who empowers us to overcome self, and our character defects and sins. If you have not been born again and converted, ask God to give you the new birth experience. Tell God that you want to receive His Son Jesus to come and live His life in you and through you. And ask Jesus to give you His Holy Spirit. And then be *willing to yield* to Him so that He can take control of your spirit, and help you to have a right spirit and a better life.

God will not make the slightest compromise with sin, and neither should we. But some people make excuses for sin and for their bad habits as if God does not have the power to give them the victory over them. These dear souls seem to believe that satan is more powerful than God. They seem to think that the devil can get them to sin, but that God doesn't have the power to keep them from sinning. They have the form of godliness but deny the power. They call themselves Christians, but they don't believe in the power of the God that they claim to serve and believe in. But in Jude 24 it states: **"God is able to keep us from falling" (sinning).**

Now is the time to overcome our defects of character and our sins. Because once probation closes it will be too late to change.

In Revelations 22:11, 12 it tell us that when Jesus returns **"he that is unjust will be unjust still, and he which is filthy, let him be filthy still, and he which is righteous let him be righteous still, and he which is holy, let him be**

holy still." In other words, once probation closes, the way your character is, is the way it will be for eternity. Now is the time for us to have a character transformation. Some people have joined the church, but they have never joined Christ. The way their character was when they joined the church is the same way today even after many years of being in the church. They have failed to advance in their Christian walk. But we must *advance*. Our characters are to be conformed to the image of Christ and not to have the worldly mold. The longer we are in the church, the more our characters should become more like Christ because when He returns, He is returning for a people who are like Him in character.

I John 3:2 states**: "Beloved, now are we the sons of God, and it does not yet appear what we shall be; but we know that when He (Jesus) shall appear, <u>we shall be like Him</u>; for we shall see Him as He is."** This is a very important and clear verse, because it is letting us know that *now* is the time that our characters must be transformed into the image of Christ because when He returns we shall be like Him if we expect to live with Him in Heaven.

It's unfortunate that some people do not believe that we can be like Jesus. But to be a Christian means to *"be Christ-like!"*And if we allow ourselves to die to self and die to our old, sin natures, and allow Christ to come abide and live in us; He will make us like Himself, and we will reflect His character and His holy image.

As we look in faith to Jesus, and behold Him by meditating on Him and by dwelling on His perfect character by studying His Holy Word, His image will be engraved on our heart, and we will be transformed in character.

To be a Christian means to be Christ-like; to treat others right; to be unselfish; to do good and kind deeds for others; like Jesus did.

According to I Corinthians 15: 53, 54, **when Jesus returns we will receive new glorious bodies,** but we will not receive new characters. And the only thing we can take to heaven is our characters. God wants to transform our characters now so that we can have the holy character traits like God has as mentioned in Galatians 5: 22, 23: **love, peace, joy, meekness, gentleness, goodness, faith, longsuffering, and self-control.**

Are you developing a character God will approve? Now is the time of probation that is given us that we may perfect a character fit for eternity. Jesus is coming soon.

When Jesus comes He is not going to cleanse us of our sins, or remove from us our defects in our characters. These things must be done for us now, before Jesus returns. When Jesus comes, those who are righteous and holy will be righteous and holy still. But those who are unrighteous, unsanctified, and filthy will remain so forever.

In Matthew chapter 25:1-13, there is an important parable about the ten virgins. **"Then shall the kingdom of heaven be likened unto ten virgins, which took their lamps, and went forth to meet the bridegroom. And five of them were wise, and five were foolish. They that were foolish took their lamps, and took no oil in them: but the wise took oil in their vessels with their lamps. While the bridegroom tarried, they all slumbered and slept. And at midnight there was a cry made, Behold, the bridegroom come; go ye out to meet him. Then all those virgins arose, and trimmed their lamps. And the foolish said unto the wise, Give us of your oil; for our lamps are gone out. But the wise answered, saying, Not so; lest there be not enough for us and you: but go ye rather to them that sell, and buy for yourselves. And while they went to buy, the bridegroom came; and they that were ready went in with him to the marriage; and the door was shut. Afterward came also the other virgins, saying Lord, Lord, open to us. But he answered and said, Verily I say unto you, I know you not. Watch therefore, for ye know neither the day nor the hour wherein the Son of man cometh."**

Notice that the wise and foolish virgins represent the two different classes of Christians within the church, and the two conditions they are in. Please also notice that the only similarity between the wise and the fool virgins is that they both have a lamp. The lamp represents the Bible. So they both have the Word of God. However, only the wise virgins have oil in their lamps. The oil represents the Holy Spirit. Also notice that the wise virgins have the Holy Spirit not only in their lamps/ Bibles, but the wise virgins also have the Holy Spirit/oil within their VESSELS also. And their vessels represent themselves. On the other hand, the foolish virgins only have the Holy Spirit/oil in their Bibles, but not within themselves! But it won't do us any good just to have the Holy Spirit in our Bibles. We must have the Holy Spirit dwelling inside of us! Having the Holy Spirit within the wise virgins meant they had allowed Jesus, through the person of His Holy Spirit to come and live His life through them, and to mold their characters into the likeness of Christ's character. That's why when Jesus came He took the wise virgins because they reflected His character and this is why He recognized them as His own. But He did not recognize the foolish virgins because they had not had a "character transformation. They did not have Christ's righteousness by faith. They had not put on Christ's white Robe of character. They still had on their own garments of self-righteousness, which are filthy rags. This is why Jesus said, "I know you not.

Beloved Reader, have you truly been born again, and have you allowed Jesus to come live His life through you in the person of His Holy Spirit? Have you allowed Him to transform your character whereby your character traits reflect Christ's character traits? Are you relying on Christ's merits and His righteous life to live through you, or are you standing in your own self-righteous goodness? Has your character changed since you accepted Christ, or do you still talk and act the same way you did before you came to Christ? Has there been a complete change in you, and are you a totally new creature in Christ? Or just half-converted? Have you advanced since you became a child of God? These are some crucial questions we need to ask ourselves.

Jesus welcomed the wise virgins because they reflected His character and they were like Him because they had His Holy Spirit within Him. However, He rejected the foolish virgins because they did not have the likeness of His character traits. They had not had a total character transformation. We must make sure that we have been totally converted, because when Jesus comes many who think they are in a saved condition will be found wanting and rejected by Christ, and He will say to them, **"Depart from me ye worker of iniquity. I never knew you."** Let us pray and ask God to help us not be among that group who will hear these solemn words from Jesus.

"The class represented by the foolish virgins are not hypocrites. They have a regard for the truth...They receive the word with readiness, but they fail of assimilating its principles...They have been content with a superficial work. They do not know God. They have not studied His character; they have not held communion with Him; therefore they do not know how to trust, how to look and live. Their service to God degenerates into a form." (*Christ Object Lessons, pp. 411, 420*)

"....We are now in God's workshop. Many of us are rough stones from the quarry. But as we lay hold upon the truth of God, its influence affects us. It elevates us and removes from us every imperfection and sin, of whatever nature. Thus we are prepared to see the King in His beauty and finally to unite with the pure and heavenly angels in the kingdom of glory. It is here that this work is to be accomplished for us, here that our bodies and spirits are to be fitted for immortality."(*Christ Object Lessons, p. 62*)

Die to self and be born again and converted

Christ cannot live in our old nature of sin; this is why we must die to self, and to our old sin nature, and be born again. God does not just want to save us from sins, but *from the very nature of sin itself,* so He can give us the new spiritual nature of Christ. This is what the new birth is about. It is a spiritual birth, but first self must die.

"In order to yield ourselves fully to Christ, self must die, and Christ must take possession of the soul temple. "When we surrender to Him, and Christ takes possession of our minds, He gives us a new heart. What is the new heart? It is the new mind. What is the mind? It is the will. Where is your will? It is either on satan's side or Christ's side. Now it is up to you. Will you put your will today on Christ's side? Jesus said: **"A new heart (mind) will I give thee."...** "Be reconciled to God. Die to self and to your old sin nature and be born again and converted. *A true conversion drives the evil demon out.*" (*Messages to Young People, MYP, vol. 1, p. 320*)

"By Contrast, (on the other hand), satan's control is brought about not by repentance and confession and surrender to God, but by surrendering more and more to the things of the world." (*Testimonies to the Church, vol. 2, p. 83*)

True Character Building

Now is the time to build characters for heaven, because it is only our characters that we can take to Heaven. We all need to have a noble Christian character.

"A pure and noble character is brought about through submission to the control of God, in conversion, and then, through grace, is earned by individual effort.

"...It is God's desire that we reflect His character. When He created us we were created in His image. He wants to restore His image and lovely character traits within us.

"But Christ has given us no assurance that to attain perfection of character is an easy matter. A noble, all-round character is not inherited. It does not come by accident. It is earned by individual effort through the merits and grace of Christ. It is formed by stern battles with self. Conflict after conflict must be waged against hereditary tendencies. We shall have to criticize ourselves closely, and allow not one unfavorable trait to remain uncorrected." (*Christ Object Lessons, p. 331)*

"We can remedy our defects of character. The possibility lies in our own will. The real difficulty arises from the corruption of an unsanctified heart, and an unwillingness to submit to the control of God. Character does not come by chance...Right character can be formed only by persevering untiring effort...*The formation of a right character is the work of a lifetime...* The conversation we have by the fireside, the books we read, the business we transact, the (programs we watch on TV), are all agents in forming our characters, and day by day decide our eternal destiny."(*My Life Today, p. 267)*

When we are born again, a new spiritual nature is imparted. And we are renewed after the image of Christ in righteousness, and holiness.

- "Character is revealed, not by occasional good deeds and occasional misdeeds, but by the tendency of the habitual words and acts." (*Steps to Christ, SC, pp. 57, 58*).
  "Thus actions repeated form habits, habits form character, and by the character our

destiny for time and eternity is decided."
(Christ Object Lessons, COL, p. 356).

- We can go to church and call ourselves Christians, but it is *character* that will determine our destiny, and whether we will end up in heaven or hell.

- "Even your thoughts must be brought into subjection to the will of God, and your feelings under the control of reason and religion. Your imagination was not given you to be allowed to run riot and have its own way without any effort at restraint or discipline. If the thoughts are wrong, the feelings will go wrong, and the thoughts and the feelings combined make up the moral character." (*5 Testimonies to the Church, p. 310)*

- "Moral perfection is required of all. Never should we lower the standard of righteousness in order to accommodate inherited and cultivated tendencies to wrong-doing. We need to understand that imperfection of character is sin." (*COL 330)*

- "No one can enter the city of God who has not knowledge of genuine conversion. In true conversion, the soul is born again. A new spirit takes possession of the temple of the soul. A new life begins. Christianity is revealed in the character." *(Review and Herald 7-30-1901)* *

- "Men may now excuse their defects of character, but in that day they will offer no excuse." (*COL 317*)

The Christian religion means more than the forgiveness of sins; it means *taking away our sins,* and filling us with the fruits, (character traits) of Jesus. *Now*, is the time that we must have character transformations into the likeness of Christ's character. There will be no change of our characters after Jesus comes. We must allow Him to change us *now!* The only thing that we will receive when Jesus comes, are glorious new bodies that will never get sick; but our characters will remain the same. *Now* is the time that we must be *transformed from sinners into saints,* and into *real Christians!* Please, thoughtfully, consider the words to this poem.

WILL THE REAL CHRISTIAN PLEASE STAND UP?

Many call themselves Christians
But they don't live up to the Name they claim.
By their words and actions they put Jesus to
Shame.
But now is not the time to be playing church and
Pretending.
Jesus is coming soon and this sinful world will be
Ending.
Many who profess to be Christians like to talk
About others behind their back.
But gossiping is a sin, yet they ignore this
Important fact.
And some are hypocrites who like to judge
Everybody else.
When they don't practice what they preach
Themselves.
And some are cold as ice.
But Christians should be loving, kind, and nice.
And some even lie, steal, and cheat.
But Christians should be the most honest people
You meet.
And some you wouldn't even know they were
Christians unless you saw them worshipping in a
Church.
Because of all the people that they hurt,
And how they act outside the church.
But true Christianity is not just a profession of
Faith.
It is a holy lifestyle we must live day by day.

It's not what you say, but what you say and do-
That proves if you are a Christian true.
God is looking for some real Christians
And He will not give up.
That's why I'm asking you today,
Will the real Christian please stand up?
Stand up and live the true Christian life!
Stand up and make a complete sacrifice!
Stand up for the truth!
And for what you know is right to do!
**WILL THE REAL CHRISTIAN PLEASE
STAND UP!**

Chapter
5

The Way I Became Born Again

Before I tell you how to have the new birth experience, first, I wish to share with you about how I, myself, became born again and converted. Because it wasn't until I had the new birth experience, that my feelings of depression, fear, and guilt went away.

For almost 20 years, I had labored for the Lord as a soul winner, but was unaware of my own lost condition. It was not until in 2012 when God led me to move to Tuskegee, Alabama to do some of my literature evangelism, when God began working on my mind to reveal to me my true unsaved condition.

All those years that I had served as a literature evangelist and Bible worker, the devil had me deceived into believing that I was in a saved condition, while I was lost—lost in the church. I wondered how God could have even used me as a worker in His vineyard, but then I thought about the experience of Peter. Peter was also a disciple that God used even before Peter had been born again and converted. Peter had performed miracles and did many good works also, but later he denied His Lord, Jesus three times. It was not until after he denied Christ that

Peter's eyes were opened to see his own true lost condition.

It was shocking to me that all those years I had been in the church, and had worked for God; however, I only had self-righteousness; and not righteousness by faith. I was only a mere moralist. I was a modern-day Pharisee, a Nicodemus. I was in a lukewarm condition. Due to all my Bible knowledge, I thought I was in need of nothing, but I was spiritually bankrupt of the Holy Spirit. Jesus was not in my heart. He was still standing outside the door to my heart wooing me, calling me, pleading and knocking for entrance into my heart. This is why I was having a roller-coaster experience, sinning and confessing, sinning and repenting over and over again, instead of having total victory over my sins and wrong habits.

I also needed to have God's love in my heart, and not just human love, which can be selfish. I needed to have Jesus' Holy Spirit living within me, controlling me, and enabling me to have victory over SELF. However, before Jesus could come into my heart, I had some rubbish in front of my heart that needed to be removed, before Jesus could come in and take His rightful place on the throne of my heart. The rubbish that was blocking Jesus from entering my heart was pride, self-righteousness, self-sufficiency and going my own way, impatience, resentment of others when they mistreated me, and irritability.

It's interesting how God used an unlikely source to reveal to me my lost condition. It happened one night when I called my best girlfriend, named Fana, who's now deceased, Fana was the type of Christian who lived her life based on the Bible. She did not just talk the Christian talk, but she lived the Christian life, and walked like Jesus. Fana was the type of friend that I could tell anything, even my secrets, and she would not broadcast my business to others, nor would she judge me. Likewise, I believe she felt the same about me, because we talked about almost anything.

Fana was actually more like a sister rather than a friend. Anyway, during one of our phone conversations, she informed me that her husband was not happy with me because I had sent her some dolls. You see, my dear friend, Fana had kidney problems, and she was unable to have a baby. Yet, having a baby seemed to be constantly on her mind. I cannot recall anytime that we talked, that she did not mention her strong desire to have her own child.

Anyway, prior to this conversation, she and I had spoken about a month earlier and I told her I was going to send her a surprise gift. Unbeknownst to her, the gift was a box of life-size, life-like baby dolls. I had hoped that by her holding the dolls, they would somehow bring her some comfort. However, just prior to sending the gift, I spoke to her husband on the phone and asked his opinion, and he told me not to bother sending the dolls because he had a special surprise that he was working on for Fana. Then, I asked him was it adoption? Were he and Fana planning to adopt a baby? This was the only thing I could think of that she and I had discussed the possibility of them doing. However, he would not tell me what his surprise was going to be.

A month passed, and during my conversations with Fana, she still never mentioned any adoption, or any surprise from her husband, so I came to the conclusion that he had forgotten about his surprise for her. Therefore, I reasoned that my surprise should not interfere with him surprising her also, so I sent the gift of dolls to her.

Nevertheless, during our latest conversation, Fana revealed to me that her husband was upset that I sent the dolls to her. I apologized, but I became very emotional and defensive. I even raised my voice to try to explain myself, and I must have sounded un-Christ like because Fana said to me, "My dear sister, Ruth, lower your voice." Then as I continued to explain, Fana said, "Ruth, you sound like you have a wrong spirit, and not the patient Spirit of Christ." So, I apologized to her, and asked her to tell her husband that I was sorry for sending the dolls, and that I did not mean to cause any problems.

After our conversation ended, I felt really bad; not because she reproved me, but because the Holy Spirit was using her words to convict me. Her words pierced my heart like a dagger. They caused me to begin examining myself, and to question my own spiritual condition. Even I did not understand why I had not kept myself under control. I wondered why I had lost my temper and tried to excuse myself and justify my wrong behavior. I knew I had to humble myself and take Fana's reproof with a right spirit, because I knew that she was telling me the truth. It was her reproof that began to cause me to think, and that set things in motion, which caused me to ask myself, "What spirit was controlling me on a moment by moment, day to day basis?" I began to wonder why sometimes I remained calm when provoked; then other times, I would lose my temper. I wondered why some times I was patient, and other times I easily lost my patience. As a consequence, I asked God to show me my real self, and to reveal to me if I had truly been born again or not.

It was about this time that I came across the books: *What Must I Do to Inherit Eternal Life* by Margaret Davis, and *His Robe or Mine,* by Frank Phillips. I think these are some of the best books written on how to die to self, how to have the new birth experience, and righteousness by faith. I began to read these books, along with the Holy Bible. I began studying everything I could on how to be born again, how to have victory over sin, how to have Christ abiding in me, and I in Him, and how to have righteousness by faith.

As I studied, I was beginning to learn the science of salvation.

I wanted to give my whole heart to Jesus, including my sins of the heart, such as resentment, impatience, and self-righteousness. I did not want anything to stand in the way of Jesus coming into my heart, because He will not share a divided heart with self, or with the devil. For the first time in my life, I began to make my getting acquainted with God a *top priority* by starting to take *"prayer walks."*

Every morning I got up early around 6:00 a.m. to take a prayer walk. These prayer walks were my pilgrimage to the cross to die to self and be crucified with Christ. I began to sit at the feet of Jesus and commune with God through nature. I did this because this is what Jesus did. He would leave the noise and distractions all around Him and go up to some desolate hill or mountain to pray. Jesus went out in nature to commune with His Father, the God of nature. And during these solemn times as I prostrated myself in the dirt and grass of the ground, and I lifted up my heart to God in prayer. John 17:3 tells us that **"This is life eternal that they might *know* Thee, the only true God, and Jesus Christ, whom Thou hast sent."** Somehow I knew based on this verse that if I wanted to have eternal life I needed to get to know God and Jesus, His Son, and that by getting acquainted with them, I would be beholding their character, and as a result by beholding, I would be changed into the same image.

I highly recommend spending time with God in nature by taking prayer walks. I spent hours in prayer and weeping to God. For the first time in my life, I was not just praying little five and ten minute prayers, but I was really yearning to know God. As I reached out to God, I was beginning to discover that I was in a lost condition. I had not really known God intimately. This was my Gethsemane experience. As Jesus wept to the Heavenly Father to be delivered from going to the cross, I prayed and wept for Jesus to deliver me from my wrong habits and sins. How few know what it is to *wrestle* with God in prayer. My Prayer went something like this:

Dear Heavenly Father, Most High God, please forgive me for my sins. (Then I confessed my sins as they came to my remembrance). Please forgive me for every wrong word, thought, and action. Please, Lord, take my heart and take my heart sins, such as resentment, impatience, irritability, pride, self-righteousness, and evil surmising. Please give me a new heart and give me the new, spiritual mind of Christ. Please, help me to love You more than sinning. Take away my filthy rags of self-righteousness, and clothe me in the white spotless Robe of Your Son, Jesus Christ's righteousness, which is His spotless character. Lord, I'm tired of sinning and confessing, sinning and repenting. Help me to hate sin like You hate sin, and please give me the victory over self, selfishness and sin. Please let Your Son, Jesus Christ come live His perfect life in and through me, and please give me Your Holy Spirit. Help me to yield to Him so He can give me the power to resist temptation and sin. Please help me to let Your Son, Jesus abide in me moment by moment, and I in Him, and Help me to submit to you, God, and to resist the devil. Help me to listen and obey Your voice, and not listen to or obey the devil. Please, also help me to bear the fruits of Your holy spirit and use Your methods in dealing with people and circumstances, instead of using the devil's methods. I choose You, Heavenly Father to be my God, and I choose Your Son, Jesus Christ to be my Lord, Savior, and Master. In the holy name of Your dear Son, Jesus Christ, I pray, amen.

For the first time I was seeking God as if for dear life; seeking Him with my whole heart and with unreserved surrender. I also began to read the Bible like I had never read it before. I dug down deep into the truths of Scripture as if seeking for gold in a buried treasure chest. I was no longer a surface-reader. After fervent and diligent prayer, I finally got my break-through.

By becoming acquainted with Christ, I hoped to become like Him. One day while outside praying and kneeling in the grass under the heat of the summer morning blue sky, I felt that God was pouring His awesome spirit of love, joy, and peace into my empty, barren heart. As I continued day by day to commune with God, I began to have this overwhelming love for God, and for other people that I had never experienced before. The love I had for people before was just human love, which can be selfish; however, this love was more extreme. This love was *divine and supernatural,* because it emanated from the heart of God, the ultimate source of love. No one can love like God can love, and when He put His love into my heart it bubbled up like a smoldering volcano ready to erupt, and I wanted to pour it out upon everyone I met in acts of love and kindness.

After I had the new birth experience, I noticed that when interacting with people, I found that the things that used to irritate me did not irritate me anymore. I was finally dead to self. But like the Apostle Paul I needed to learn how to die daily. You see, a dead man cannot be irritated or hurt at all. I was learning to die to my old sin nature, and I was being converted (changed) into the likeness of Christ in character.

When people spoke to me in a rough tone, or were disrespectful to me, it used to bother me, but I did not recognize this new me who could take people's abuse without it upsetting me. Instead of wanting to defend myself, instead of getting angry, instead of wanting to retaliate, instead of getting resentful, I had the attitude: "Forgive them Father, for they know not what they do." I began to look at people through the loving eyes of Jesus; I began to only want to seek the good of others, instead of selfishly looking out for my own self anymore. I looked for ways to bless people and make their lives easier. Instead of getting impatient and losing my temper like I used to, this new creature that God had transformed me into was calm and I could take abuse from people with a right spirit of love, peace, forgiveness, and patience.

I looked for ways to show God's love to my fellow mankind. I looked for opportunities to live God's love. If people shouted at me rudely, as long as I chose to yield to the power of the Holy Spirit, I could take it patiently without the slightest irritation, or feeling of retaliation. I began to see people who hurt me, instead of as my enemy, as precious souls that Jesus died for. It was at this time that I even began to say to almost everyone I met when I departed from them, "I love you in Jesus!"

I finally had the supernatural love of God in my heart and I wanted everyone I met to experience a little of His love just by coming into contact with me. And when I was tempted to lose my temper, I was learning to quickly yield up to the Holy Spirit to control me instead, of yielding down to my old animal, sin nature. And this is a definite indicator that you have been born again, and that is you will have God's overwhelming love in your heart for Him and for others.

It amazes me when some Christians look at me in unbelief when I tell them that we can have victory over sin. They seem to believe that the devil can cause them to sin, but that God does not have the power to keep them from falling or sinning as He promised in Jude 24. However, Jesus did not come to save us *in* sin, but FROM our sins, according to Matthew 1:29 it states: **"Behold the Lamb of God, which takes away the sin of the world."**

The gospel is power, beloved. Many people don't want to become Christians because they see so many professed Christians living such weak sin-filled lives with no power, and no victory over sin. However, we who claim to be the followers of Christ must not just have the form of godliness while denying the power, but we must start claiming God's power to give us the victory over sin. The Christian life is a life of freedom in Jesus, not bondage. Christianity is not just a theory like evolution. It is a living principle. I praise God that I finally learned how to be truly born again and allow God's Holy Spirit power to work through me to empower me to overcome sin in my life.

What Does It Mean to Be Born Again?

- "When the Spirit of God takes possession of the heart, it transforms the life... The blessing comes when by faith the soul surrenders itself to God. Then that power which no human eye can see creates a new being in the image of God...Then the Spirit of God through faith produces a new life in the soul." (*Desire of Ages, pp. 175, 176*)

The new birth experience requires a complete surrender, a dying to self, before a new creature can be born anew by the power of God. We had no choice in the first physical birth, but the new spiritual birth must be by our choice. Once we let go of our own delusions of wanting to be in control of self, and we become willing to give up self, then a power is activated within us enabling us to overcome sin, but only as we yield to that power, which is the power of the Holy Spirit.

Being born again means being willing to get off the throne of your life and let Jesus take His rightful place on the throne of our hearts. Is God calling the shots in your life, or are you working independent of Him and His will? Please consider the following essential quotes below concerning the new birth experience.

When you are Born Again, Jesus Will Live in You and Empower You

- **"For I am not ashamed of the gospel of Christ; for it is the power of God unto salvation to everyone that believeth"** Romans 1:6.

- **"As many as received him, to them gave he power to become the sons of**

God, even to them that believe in his name" John 1:12.

- 'This power is not in the human agent. It is the power of God. When a soul receives Christ, he receives power to live the life of Christ." (*Christ Object Lessons, COL, p. 314*)

- "Gospel religion is Christ in the life – a living, active principle. It is the grace of Christ revealed in character and wrought out in good works." (*COL, p. 384*)

- "It is no more we that live, but Christ that lives in us, and He is the hope of glory. Self is dead, but Christ is a living Saviour." (*Testimonies to Ministers, TM p. 389*)

- **"Now the God of peace…make you perfect in every good work to do his will, working in you that which is pleasing in his sight, through Jesus Christ"** Hebrews 13:20, 21.

- "All must obtain a living experience for themselves; they must have Christ enshrined in the heart, His Spirit controlling the affections, or their profession of faith is of no value, and their condition will be even worse than if they had never heard the truth. " *(5 Testimonies to the Church, p. 619)*

- "May the Lord help us to die to self and be born again, that Christ may live in us, a living, active principle, and a power that will keep us holy." *(9 Testimonies p. 188)*

What an awesome honor and privilege to actually have God living within us! Jesus wants us to allow Him to live in us daily so that we will be able to have the fruit of the Holy Spirit in our lives, and represent His character to others. God wants us live the fruits of His character in our daily lives, which are love, peace, joy, meekness, goodness, faithfulness, gentleness, long suffering, and self-control. The outline below helped me to be born again and to understand the science of salvation.

In order to have the new birth experience, you need to confess and forsake your sins. Ask God to bring them to your remembrance. You will not remember every sin, but confess the ones you remember. Try to be as specific as possible. If you have ever stolen, told a lie, or any sins, confess them. Then ask God for forgiveness and to help you turn away from committing those sins again. When you have committed a sin, never make excuses, because when we make excuses for our sins, we are cherishing them. Also, when you sin, do not blame others for causing you to sin, because this is not sincere repentance, but it is worldly repentance.

In order to establish a close relationship with God, take time to get to know God, because to know Him is to love Him, then you will want to stop sinning and hurting Him. When you love someone you won't want to hurt them. Jesus obeyed His Heavenly Father unconditionally, because He loved Him unconditionally. You cannot obey God without first establishing a love relationship with God; otherwise, trying to obey Him will be a burden. However, when you learn to love God, then obeying Him and pleasing Him will be a joy and a pleasure. As you study God's character by studying His Word, you will behold His loving character, and by beholding Him, you will become changed into His image of love, peacefulness, patience, and meekness.

I had to learn to love and trust God. When we sin, it is because we love self, or we love some cherished sin more than God. After I got to know God intimately it became a joy to obey Him because I knew He only had my best interest at heart. The things that God did not want me to do were only hurtful to me. God does not tell us not to do things because He's trying to be restrictive, but because He loves us and wants to protect us. Behold Jesus. We behold Him in our quiet times of prayer, and in our solemn times of studying the holy Bible. When you love God, then you will trust Him explicitly to know what is best for you.

Spend time with God and with Jesus. One way that you can take the time to establish a personal and intimate relationship with God, your Creator, and with His Lovely Son, Jesus Christ by taking *"prayer walks,"* and communing with God through nature. This is what Jesus did. He left the crowds and spent time on the hill-tops in solitude with just Him and His Heavenly Father. Go into your closet or bedroom alone and prostrate and bow yourself down low and yield up your heart to God in prayer. Sincerely plead with Him to give you the gift of repentance, the gift of salvation, the gift of faith, the gift of His Son, Jesus Christ to come live in you, the gift of His Holy Spirit and His grace to come dwell in you to give you the power to resist the temptation to sin. Seek God with your whole heart, holding back nothing. He said if you seek Him with your whole heart, you will find Him. And you cannot seek Him with your whole heart with a little five or ten minute prayer.

You must spend quality time with God. This is with any relationship. No good relationship between two people can be formed unless they first spend quality time together getting acquainted. If you take some prayer walks out in nature, take the time to appreciate the beauty of God's creation. As you behold the beauty of nature, you will be beholding the beauty of God because in every green blade of grass, in every beautiful flower, in every soft flower petal, in every gentle breeze, in every warm ray of sunshine upon your face, in every bright blue sky, in every majestic tall tree, these all attest to the proof of God's love. As you take your prayer walk, start praising God for the beauty of the nature that God has created. Praise Him for the trees, the flowers, the grass, the air, the blue sky, the breeze, the sun on your face, and for the birds, and so forth.

Chapter
6

The Way to Have the
New Birth Experience

What is the *New Birth* experience, and how can you have it?

You may to do the following things that I did to be born again:

1. Confess your sins and determine to forsake them.

2. Ask God to put His love into your heart for Him and for your fellow mankind. Ask God to remove selfishness so that you will love Him more than your sins and bad habits.

3. Spend quality time having morning and evening devotion. During devotion, read God's holy Word. Through studying the Holy Bible you will learn God's Will for your life. Study Jesus' parables and the deep lessons He teaches us through them. Study Jesus' character and how He dealt with people with kindness, love,

compassion, patience, and peacefulness. Then, ask God to mold your character into the likeness of His character.

4. Don't just read, but *study* the Bible. **"Study to show thyself approved. A workman that needeth not to be ashamed, rightly dividing the truth"** II Timothy 2:15. The opposite is also true. You will not be approved by God if you do not study His Word. How will you know His Will if you don't study His Word to see what He has to say to you?

5. Study the Holy Bible at least one hour per day. At first, it may be very difficult, or maybe even boring. The devil will not make it easy for you to draw close to God. The devil will try to block you from forming a relationship with God. Therefore, you will have to put forth effort to form this relationship with your Creator. The more you draw closer to God the closer you will want to draw to Him. We make time for what we want to make time for, and for the things we consider important, so make time for God. Make Him a *priority*, because He is more important than anything else. Some times during my morning and evening devotion times with God, I take my hymn

book and serenade God by singing to Him sacred hymns.

6. When you learn to die to self, you can only keep the old, selfish and proud sin nature; and *self dead* by continuing to *yield* yourself up moment-by-moment to the power of the Holy Spirit, instead of yielding down to your old, carnal, fleshly, animal, lower, sin nature.

In John 3: 5, Jesus said, **"You must be born again. Except a man be born again he cannot see the Kingdom of Heaven."**
To be a Christian means to be like Christ. It is a godly life alone that God will approve. You can know if you have been truly born again. You can know if you have Christ abiding in you. Matthew 7:16 says: **"By their *fruits* you shall know them."**
Once we are born again our character and behavior will exhibit the character of Christ, and we will bear or have the fruits and graces of the Holy Spirit expressed in our character.

What are the graces, or characteristics, or fruits of the Holy Spirit?
They are found in Galatians 5:22, 23, and they are: **Love, joy, peace, goodness, meekness, faith, gentleness, long suffering, and self-control, which means temperance or patience.** Each of these character traits represents God's

true character traits. When you are born again, you too will express *all* of these traits in your character. Does your character and behavior show you to be a loving, peaceful, patient, good, gentle, and meek person who has self-control? And I'm not talking about just when things are going well, but how do you act when things are going wrong? Anybody can be peaceful and have a right spirit when things are going right. But do you allow the Holy Spirit to control your spirit when things are not going right?

When we are truly born again and converted, and when we live by faith that we have Christ and His Holy Spirit living within us, then, the *fruits of the Holy Spirit* will be seen in our life. And if you stay *yielded* to the Holy Spirit to control you, He will give you the fruits or character traits of God as you need them and when you need them.

For instance, when you need patience, if you yield yourself up to the Holy Spirit, and if He is abiding in you, He will work in you patience when you need it. And when you need self-control, He will work in you and help you to have self control. But you have to *yield* up to Him, and allow Him to control your spirit, and help you to have a right spirit when dealing with people, or difficult circumstances. If you lose your temper, this shows that you are not yielded self to the power of the Holy Spirit to control you.

When you are born again and you have the Holy Spirit and the life of Christ in you, *you will have the love of God overflowing in your heart—not only towards God, but towards your fellow man, and your character will produce the same fruit or characteristics that were in Christ.* Does your character possess these graces and character traits mentioned in Galatians, Chapter five? Do you have genuine love for your fellow man, and do you express that love towards the people that you encounter from day-to-day? Anybody can love their family and friends, but do you have genuine love for the strangers that you might meet on a daily basis? John 13:35 tells us, **"By this shall all men know that ye are my disciples, if ye have *love* one to another."**

Ask yourself, "Just as soon as anyone crosses you, or offends you, does there arise in your heart a feeling of bitterness, a spirit of rebellion? If this is the spirit you have, bear in mind that you have not the spirit of Christ. It is another spirit. The Spirit of Christ will be revealed in all who are born of God. Strife and contention cannot arise among those who are controlled by God's Spirit." (*Thoughts from the Mount of Blessings, p. 62 or 48, 1896*)

God desires that we totally surrender ourselves to Him. But we must be willing to die to self and to our old sinful nature so that He can give us a new nature, a new disposition, a new character, and allow Him to live His holy life through us. Some people seem to want Jesus as their Saviour, but not as their Lord, because they don't want to obey Him. They like the fact that He died to pay the penalty for their sins, and thereby became their Saviour on the cross, but they don't want to obey Him as their Lord and Master.

When you become born again, you are to give all of yourself to Christ, and accept all that He offers, *including His power to obey.*

Some people desire to be born again but after they pray and ask God to come into their heart they see no change in their lives. It is because they have not surrendered their entire heart. They have not totally died to self.

To die to self means to deal with people and situations using Christ's love, or using the fruits of the Holy Spirit, and to give up the right to use satan's methods, but instead to use God's methods.

Only when the heart is emptied completely of self, then Jesus can come and abide in the heart, and the Holy Spirit can come in. Jesus will not share a divided heart with self or with satan. Jesus wants to come into our hearts, but we must first be willing to completely surrender our hearts totally to Him.

For some, Jesus can't come and abide in their heart's because they have the door to their heart blocked with things like selfishness, pride, an evil temper, some are self-sufficient instead of completely depending on God, some have impatience, lust, stubbornness, worldly ambition, love of the world, covetousness, selfishness, self-righteousness, jealousy, envy, evil-surmising, irritability, bitterness, or fault-finding, and so He can't enter their hearts.

There are those who profess to be followers of Jesus Christ who have never died to self. They have never fallen on the *Rock*, Jesus Christ and been broken of their old, lower, fallen, sin nature. They have been baptized but when they were baptized they were baptized and self was still alive. Self did not die. They did not give up all for Christ. Therefore, when they went down into the watery grave of baptism self was still alive. Instead of coming up out of the water as new creatures in Christ, they came up from the water the same as they went down into it. Jesus says: **"He who is not willing for forsake all for me is not worthy of me."**

What is Temptation?

Temptation is not sin, because the Bible says that **"Jesus was tempted in all points as we are, yet without sin"** (Hebrews 4: 14-16). Temptation is not sin; it is only the *possibility* to sin; it is the possibility of what you could do, but not what you have to do. The devil can only tempt us to sin; he cannot make us sin. It all boils down to our choice. When does temptation become sin? Is it when we succumb to the evil suggestion and act on it? No, it is when we contemplate it! **"As a man thinketh in his heart, so is he"** Proverbs 23:7. If an evil thought comes to your mind, this is not sin. It only becomes sin if you dwell on the evil thought, or if you want the evil thought and you desire it, or lust after it.

Where then, is the sin? IN the heart! To eradicate the act of sinning, we need to get a new spiritual heart, which is the new *spiritual mind* of Christ.

God Will Help You When Tempted and Make a Way of Escape

- **"There hath no temptation taken you but such as is common to man: but God is faithful, who will not suffer you to be tempted above that ye are able; but with the temptation also make a way to escape, that ye may be able to bear it"** I Corinthians 10:13.

- "Our Heavenly Father measures and weighs every trial before He permits it to come upon the believer. He considers the circumstances and the strength of the one who is to stand under the proving and test of God, and He never permits the temptation to be greater than the capacity of resistance. If the soul is overborne, and the person over-powered, this can never be charged to God,…but the one tempted was not vigilant and prayerful and did not appropriate by faith the provisions God had abundantly in store for him. Christ never failed a believer in his hour of combat. The believer must claim the promise and meet the foe in the name of the Lord." (*Our High Calling, OHC, p. 323*)

- When you are a true believer, you will not be tempted beyond what you can bear, and God also will make a way of escape, but we must take His way of escape, otherwise He cannot help us.

- "We must watch ourselves carefully. Moment by moment we must keep ourselves under the control of the Spirit of God. Watch continually unto prayer. If you will only watch, continually watch unto prayer, if you will do everything as if you were in the immediate presence of God, you will be saved from yielding to temptation, and may hope to be kept pure, spotless, and undefiled till the last." (*Gospel Workers, p. 128*)

- "Through the grace of God and their own diligent effort, they must be conquerors in the battle with evil." (*The Great Controversy, p. 425*)

- When you are tempted to sin, you will feel the temptation to react. We will feel the promptings to sin. This is why Christ's help is needed. Instantly the Holy Spirit will alert us, and if we quickly submit to God, He will then have the right to control our spirit and give us the victory. **"And thine ears shall hear a word behind thee, saying, 'This is the way, walk ye in it, when ye turn to the right hand, and when ye turn to the left"** Isaiah 30:21.

At the moment of temptation, quickly submit to God, however, He always leaves you free to choose.

- "If the voice of Jesus is not heeded at once, it becomes confused in the mind with a multitude of other voices." *(7 Bible Commentary, p. 967)*

- "We want to become so sensitive to holy influences that the lightest whisper of Jesus will move our souls." *(That I May Know Him, KH, p. 361)*

- "Conscience is the voice of God, heard amid the conflict of human passions; when it is resisted, the Spirit of God is grieved." (*5 Testimonies to the Church, p. 120)*

- "The Holy Spirit will not compel men to take a certain course of action. We are free moral agents; and when sufficient evidence has been given us as to our duty, it is left with us to decide our course." (*Fundamentals of Education, p. 124*)

Take God's Way of Escape and Submit to Him

- **Submit yourselves therefore to God. Resist the devil, and he will flee from you. Draw nigh to God, and he will draw nigh to you"** James 4: 7, 8.

- "Jesus gained the victory through submission and faith in God,...We cannot save ourselves from the tempter's power; he has conquered humanity, and when we try to stand in our own strength, we shall become a prey to his devices' but 'the name of the lord is a strong tower: the righteous runneth into it, and is safe.' Satan trembles and flees before the weakest soul who finds refuge in that mighty name." (*Desire of Ages, DA 131*)

- **"The Lord knows how to deliver the godly out of temptations"** 2 Peter 2:9.

- "As soon as we incline our will to harmonize with God's will, the grace of God stands ready to cooperate with the human agent." *(Heavenly Places, p. 27)*

- "In the whole Satanic force there is no power to overcome one soul who in simple trust casts himself on Christ." *(Christ Object Lessons, p. 157)*

- When we sense that we are being tempted to sin, we should quickly submit ourselves to God. He will then work in us whatever is needed for us to have the victory.

God Is Able to Keep You from Falling

- **"Now unto Him (God) that is able to keep you from falling (sinning), and to present you faultless before the presence of his glory with exceeding joy"** Jude 24.

- **"For, I the Lord thy God will hold thy right hand, saying unto thee, Fear not; I will help thee"** Isaiah 41:13.

- **"My grace is sufficient for thee: for my strength is made perfect in weakness"** 2 Corinthians 12:9.

- "The only hope for us if we would overcome is to unite our will to God's will and work in cooperation with Him, hour by hour and day by day." (*Thoughts from the Mount of Blessings, MB, p. 143*)

- "The Christian life is one of daily surrender, submission, and continual overcoming." (*4 Bible Commentary, p. 1154*)

- It is God's grace that gives us power to obey the laws of God.

- "Christ always separates the contrite soul from sin. He came to destroy the works of the devil, and He has made provision that the Holy Spirit shall be imparted to every repentant soul, to keep him from sinning." (*DA 311*)

- "He who has not sufficient faith in Christ to believe that He can keep him from sinning has not the faith that will give him an entrance into the kingdom of God." (*RH Review and Herald, 3-10-1905*)

What Does It Mean to Have Jesus Abide in You?

"I am the Vine, ye are the branches, he that abideth in me, and I in him, the same bringeth forth much fruit; for without me ye

can do nothing" John 15:5. We allow Christ to abide, or remain, or live in us by *yielding* ourselves completely to Him, and allowing Him to be in control. In order to stop sinning, we need to learn to allow Jesus to abide in us. What is this *fruit* that we will bear or bring forth if we allow Jesus to abide it us?

The *fruit* is the character traits of God, which are love, joy, peace, meekness, goodness, gentleness, faithfulness, long-suffering, and self-control, or patience. Jesus abided in (completely depended on God, the Father), and we must do the same and abide in Jesus. We are to receive from Jesus as He received from His Father the power to live right. Jesus could not rely on His own power. Likewise, we cannot rely on our own feeble strength to overcome.

We need the living, supernatural, divine power of Christ within us. The old nature has to completely die, and the new spiritual nature invited in to create something in us that we human beings are utterly incapable of producing within ourselves.

We were created to reflect the image of Jesus, and we can if only we permit Him to abide and live in us by the presence of His Holy Spirit. The only way we can bring forth the fruits of the Holy Spirit, love, peace, joy, meekness, gentleness, goodness, faithfulness, and self-control is to abide in the Vine, Jesus, and to have Him abiding in us.

By Allowing Jesus to Abide in Us, We Will Stop Sinning!

The following quote was taken from the book: *Branch and the Vine* by Pastor Frank Phillips.

Whosoever abideth in Him, *sinneth not*; whosoever sinneth hath not seen Him, neither known Him" I John 3:6. This abiding in Christ involves a love relationship. It is only when we *abide (yield and remain) in Christ* that we cease sinning. It's impossible for the abiding Christ to commit sin. This abiding experience results in freedom from sin. It doesn't mean temptation will disappear, nor does it mean there won't be an occasion to stumble or fall; but it does mean we are not going to deliberately turn our backs on the Lord Jesus if we are abiding in the Vine. Satan may come along with something very attractive, but if we continue abiding in the Vine, the attraction will pass—God will take responsibility for that. All the while, the character of the Lord Jesus will continue to be credited to us so long as we are abiding, even if we make an unintentional mistake. Intentional rebelliousness that proceeds out of an unborn natural heart that hasn't yet died will be past history. Jesus says that being born again and abiding will take care of this.

Abiding in Christ, He takes care of, or controls the carnal, fleshly, natural man, and helps us to keep the natural man, or our old, carnal sin nature dead. However, we must willingly die to the old, carnal, natural man to be born again to the new, spiritual man of having Christ' Holy Spirit living in us and empowering us to live the life of Christ.

When we confess and forsake our sins, then Jesus pardons us, and this is known as justification. But then, by faith, we accept His free gift of sanctification, which means, Jesus brings us into harmony with His holy law and we become in cooperation, and in harmony with His holy will, and He gives us through sanctification the gift of the power to live a holy and sanctified life. Then we can live Christ righteous life by faith. This is called having righteousness by faith, and we *surrender and allow* Jesus to come and live His righteous, pure, and sinless life in and through us moment by moment.

God wants us to have this wonderful abiding experience between ourselves and Jesus on a daily, moment by moment basis. As Pastor Meade MacGuire put it, "In this abiding experience lies our daily victory over sin, our ability to bring forth to His glory, our unlimited success in prayer, and our assurance of being ready to meet our King when He returns in glory. (*p. 88).*

What is forgiveness?

- "Forgiveness has a broader meaning than many suppose...God's forgiving is not merely a judicial act by which He sets us free from condemnation. It is not only forgiveness for sin, but *reclaiming from sin.* It is the outflow of redeeming love that transforms the heart. David had the true conception of forgiveness when he prayed, 'Create in me a clean heart, O God; and renew a right spirit within me.'" *(Thoughts from the Mount of Blessing, p. 114)*

When you are Born Again, Jesus Will Live in You and Empower You!

- **"For I am not ashamed of the gospel of Christ; for it is the *power* of God unto salvation to everyone that believeth"** Romans 1:6.

- **"As many as received him, to them gave the power to become the sons of God, even to them that believe in his name"** John 1:12.

- "This power is not in the human agent. It is the power of God. When a soul receives Christ, he receives power to live the life of Christ." *(Christ Object Lessons, COL, p. 314)*

- "When we live by faith on the Son of God, the fruits of the Holy Spirit will be seen in our life; not one will be missing. If you stay yielded to the Holy Spirit to control you, He will give you the fruits of God's character traits as you need them and when you need them." *(Steps to Christ, p. 100)*

- "When the sinner accepts Christ and lives in Him, Jesus takes his sins and weaknesses and then grafts the repentant soul into Himself, so that he sustains the relation to Christ that the branch does to the Vine. We have nothing; we are nothing, unless we receive virtue from Jesus Christ." *(That I May Know Him KH, p. 100)*

- "Gospel religion is Christ in the life – a living, active principle. It is the grace of Christ revealed in character and wrought out in good works." *(COL 384)*

- "It is no more we that live, but Christ that lives in us, and He is the hope of glory. Self is dead, but Christ is a living Saviour." *(Testimonies to Ministers, p. 389)*

- **Now the God of peace...make you *perfect* in every good work to do *his will, working in you that which is pleasing* in his sight, through Jesus Christ"** Hebrew 13:20, 21.

- "All must obtain a living experience for themselves; they must have Christ enshrined in the heart, His Spirit controlling the affections, or their profession of faith is of no value, and their condition will be even worse than if they had never heard the truth." *(5 Testimonies, p. 619)*

- "May the Lord help us to die to self and be born again, that Christ may live in us, a living, active principle; a power that will keep us holy." (*9 Testimonies to the Church, p. 188)*

Only We Can Break the Connection
   In order to have victory over self, the devil, and sin, we must remain vitally connected to Jesus, the Vine moment-by-moment. However, if we *choose* to sin, then we break our connection with Him.

- "God gives us strength, reasoning power, time, in order that we may build characters on which He can place His stamp of approval. He desires each child of His to build a noble character by the doing of pure noble deeds. In our character building we must build on Christ because He is the sure foundation—a foundation which can never be moved." (*Steps to Christ, SC, p. 155)*

"**That ye put off concerning the former conversation the old man which is corrupt according to the deceitful lusts; and be renewed in the spirit of your mind; and that ye put on the new man, which after God is created in righteousness and true holiness**" Ephesians 4: 22-24.

What Does it Mean to Be Converted?

"Conversion means to be changed. "Conversion is a work that most do not appreciate. It is not a small matter to transform an earthly, sin-loving mind and bring it to understand the unspeakable love of Christ, the charms of His grace, and the Excellency of God, so that the soul shall be imbued with diving love and captivated with the heavenly mysteries. When he understands these things, his former life appears disgusting and hateful. He hates sin, and breaking his heart before God, he embraces Christ as the life and joy of the soul. He renounces his former pleasures. He has a new mind, new affections, new interest, new will; his sorrows, and desires, and love are all new...Heaven which once possessed no charms, is now viewed in its riches and glory; and he contemplates it as his future home, where he shall see, love, and praise the One who hath redeemed him by His precious blood. The works of holiness which once appeared wearisome are now his delight. The Word of God, which was dull and uninteresting, is now chosen as his study, the man of his counsel. It is a letter written to him from God, bearing the inscription of the Eternal. All need to understand the process of conversion. The fruit is seen in the changed life."(*Steps to Christ, pp. 121, 122*)

It is unfortunate that some people who profess to be Christians say they have no self-control. However, one of the *fruits of the Holy Spirit* that we receive when we are born again is temperance or self-control. So if someone lacks self-control they need to be born again so that they will have the fruit of the Holy Spirit, self-control. Some seem to want Justification, which is their title to heaven. But they don't want Sanctification, which is our fitness to live in heaven. But we need both. We need to be justified which means to be forgiven and pardoned for our sins.

John 17:17 states: **"Sanctify them by Thy Truth. Thy Word is Truth."** We are sanctified by *obeying* God's Word, which is the Word of Truth. Sanctification means to live by **"every word that proceeds from the mouth of God."** If you're living a life of disobedience, and a life that is contrary to the Word of God you are not sanctified.

"It is through the truth, by the power of the Holy Spirit, that we are to be sanctified-transformed into the likeness of Christ. And in order for this change to be wrought in us, there must be an unconditional, wholehearted acceptance of the truth, and unreserved surrender of the soul to its transforming power.

"Many persons cling tenaciously to their peculiarities. Even after they profess to accept the truth, to yield themselves to Christ, the same old habits are indulged, the same self-esteem manifested, the same false notions entertained. Although such ones claim to be converted, it is evident that they have not yielded themselves to the transforming power of the truth...

"The new birth consists in having new motives, new tastes, and new tendencies. Those who are begotten unto a new life by the Holy Spirit have become partakers of the divine nature, and in all their habits and practices, they will give evidence of their relationship to Christ." (*Our High Calling, OHC, p. 120*)

"He who feels whole, and who thinks that he is reasonably good, and is contented with his condition, does not seek to become a partaker of the grace and righteousness of Christ. Pride feels no need, and so it closed the heart against Christ and the infinite blessing He came to give. There is not room for Jesus in the heart of such a person. Those who are rich and honorable in their own eyes do not ask in faith, and receive the blessing of God. They feel that they are full, therefore they go away empty. Those who know that they cannot possibly save themselves, or of themselves do any righteous action, are the ones who appreciate the help that Christ can bestow. They are the poor in spirit, whom He declares to be blessed." (*Ministry of Healing, pp. 480*, 481)

The Christian life is a constant battle. Some want to wear the cross, but don't want to bear the cross. Sanctification is a daily constant warfare between the spirit and the flesh. Sanctification is complete obedience and continual conformity to the will of God.

"True sanctification is daily dying to self and daily conforming to the will of God. We must die to our old nature of sin and become a *partaker* of Christ holy and divine nature. God can forgive us of any sin we commit, but He can't forgive us of holding on to our nature to sin because He can't do anything with it. We must get a new nature and die to the old nature that is prone to sin." *(Steps to Christ, SC, p. 86)*

Paul's sanctification was a daily conflict with self. Said he, **"I die daily"** (I Cor. 15: 31). We must learn to give up our own wisdom, our own will, and our own way, and surrender totally to God's wisdom, His will, and His way. Our attitude needs to be "Not my will Lord, but Thy Will be done." Jesus pleased the Father. We need to ask ourselves, who are we trying to please? Are we trying to please God in everything that we say or do? Or are we trying to please ourselves, or someone else?

"We cannot retain *self* and yet enter the kingdom of God. If we ever attain unto holiness, it will be through the renunciation of self and the reception of the mind of Christ." *(Testimonies to the Church, vol. 2, p. 656)*

We need justification and to be pardoned, but we also need to learn how to live the sanctified and holy life. And *holiness* means to be wholly committed to God, to live a life of purity without defiling oneself with the things of this world. It means to be separate and set apart from the world for holy use. "No one who claims holiness is really holy. Those who are registered as holy in the books of heaven are not aware of the fact, and are the last ones to boast of their own goodness.

"It is not conclusive evidence that a man is a Christian because he manifests spiritual ecstasy under extraordinary circumstances.

"*Holiness* is not rapture; it is an entire surrender of the will to God; it is living by every word that proceeds from the mouth of God; it is doing the will of our heavenly Father; it is trusting God in trial, in darkness as well as in the light; it is walking by faith and not by sight; it is relying on God with unquestioning confidence, and resting in His love…unless all selfishness is put away, unless self is crucified, we can never be holy as God is holy." (*The Great Controversy, p. 591*)

It wasn't until I was born again and converted that my life started having real joy and peace of mind.

Perhaps, if you are feeling sad, depressed, guilty, or fearful, it is because there may be some sins in your life that you need to *confess and repent of.*

What Is Confession?

To confess simply means to admit that you are guilty of sinning. It means to acknowledge that you have done wrong without making excuses or self-justification. Sincerely and humbly confess your sins and do not just say: 'Dear heavenly Father, please be merciful and forgive me for my sins. In the holy name of Your dear Son, Jesus Christ. Amen.' Try to *be specific* when you confess your sins. *Admit* when you are wrong, and ask God for forgiveness. If you make excuses for sin, or if you put the blame for your sins partly on others, then this is worldly repentance, and you are cherishing your sins, and you can't be forgiven. Therefore, first you must *acknowledge* your own guilt. Nobody *made* you sin. You *chose* to sin!

According to Isaiah 59:2 our **"sins separate us from God."** If you have sinned, ask God for forgiveness and ask Jesus to come and live in your heart.

What Is Repentance?

Repentance means to be sorry for sin, and to be sorry enough to quit. Repentance means to turn away from sin. You do not have true repentance if you ask God to forgive you but you continue to commit the same sin. **"If we confess our sins, He is faithful and just to forgive us our sins and to cleanse us from all unrighteousness"** (I John 1:9). Luke 13:3 **states: "Unless you repent you will all likewise perish or die."** Proverbs 28:13 tells us: **"He who covers his sins shall not prosper, but he that confesses and forsakes his sins shall have mercy."** Have you just confessed your sins? Or have you also forsaken them with the help of Jesus Christ and the power of His Holy Spirit?

You cannot repent without God's help because even repentance is a gift from God. So if you don't feel like repenting, ask God to give you the gift of repentance.

The words "repentance or repent" are spoken in the Holy Bible over 75 times! Therefore, it must be important.

Some people only repent out of a sense of selfishness. They are not genuinely sorry for their sins. They just tell God they are sorry because they fear the punishment for their sins. But genuine sincere repentance should come from a heart of sorrow. We should be sorry for our sins because we know that our sins hurt God, the Father, and hurt Jesus, and grieves the Holy Spirit, and when we sin we crucify Christ afresh.

Carefully, think about the important words of this next poem. It is my sincere hope that this poetic message blesses you, and that you will take the words to heart…

DON'T BELIEVE THE DEVIL'S BIG LIE!

I've heard it said so many times,
'Oh, we can't overcome sin in our lives.'
But this is the devil's big lie.
Listen carefully and I'll tell you why.
God's Word says we can overcome.
Victory over sin can be won.
But the power comes from within.
It is God's Holy Spirit who empowers us to
Overcome sin.
In Matthew 5: 48, it tells us to 'be perfect like our
Father in Heaven.'
So it's not impossible, my brethren.
The devil says we can't be perfect, but the devil
Is a liar.
We can be perfect if we desire!
Some people don't like the word perfect because
They don't want to obey.
They want to keep sinning and going their own
Way.
A true Christian may make a mistake and sin.
But will not deliberately live in sin because Jesus
Dwells within.

The question is not can we be perfect, but do we
Want to be?
Through God all things are possible if we
Believe!
It's sad to hear people spreading the devil's old
Lie.
That in our sins we must continue and die.
God has the power to give us the victory over
Every single sin.
If we surrender our wills and lives to Him.
In Genesis 6:9, God called Noah perfect,
And in Job 1:1, God called Job perfect, too.
So why can't He call perfect me and you?
He called them perfect because they resisted sin.
Instead of yielding to satan's temptations, they
yielded to God's Power to help them win.
God will not save us IN sins, but FROM sins.
And if we truly love Him we will forsake them.
Repeatedly, the Bible tells us to be perfect and
Overcome.
**So will you believe God's Word, or satan, the
Lying one?**

In Matthew 5:48 it states: **"Be ye
therefore perfect as your Father in heaven is
perfect."** Some seem to ignore this Scripture as
if God did not really mean for us to be perfect
and that the Bible is just joking. But no! The
Bible means what it says, and God certainly
would not give us an impossibility. God never

tells us to do something unless He makes it possible to obey.

As I'm sure you have noticed the poem you just read is about the issue of perfection. Could it possibly be the reason God inspired me to write this poem is because God is tired of people making excuses for sin, and saying that it is impossible to stop sinning?

It's unfortunate that the words "perfect" or "repent" have seemed to become dirty words in Christianity. It seems as if you even say these words you are looked upon as if you are being a fanatic, and are bordering on fanaticism. Yet, these words are mentioned in the Holy Bible over 50 times! So God doesn't have a problem with these words, or with us repenting and being perfect. He knows that when we allow His Son Jesus to live in us, we can be perfect by the power of His Holy Spirit. We can't do it in human strength. It is a *supernatural experience*. And it is not us that are perfect, but Jesus Christ dwelling within us makes us perfect.

Sadly, I have heard some professed Christians say, "But I'm only human!" But if we are only human, we are not Christians. Christians are *partakers of the divine nature*, and when Christians have Christ in them, the hope of Glory, they have a supernatural being in them, who makes them part human and part divine.

The reason I think some avoid the word "perfect" is because either they are afraid to be perfect because they think it will require them to give up something that they do not want to give up, namely "sin." Or it is because they do not understand God's definition of what it means to be perfect.

Man's definition of being perfect is flawed. When most people that I've spoken to define the word perfect or perfection, they say that it is a level of attainment in which you strive higher and higher to reach until you reach the highest level and then you will never sin again. But no, this is not God's definition of perfection. God's definition of perfection is a 'human being who has given their heart, soul, mind, and life completely to God, and they walk in daily consistent obedience to God. They walk after the Holy Spirit instead of walking after the flesh and fulfilling the desires of their old fleshly sin nature.'

This is why God called human beings like Noah and Job and others "perfect or blameless." It was because these individuals lived a life of consistent obedience. They put God's Will before their own pleasures. They could have sinned, but they chose to resist temptation and obey God instead. They did not have a roller-coaster experience like many other Christians – sinning and repenting, sinning and repenting. They learned to yield to the power of the Holy Spirit within them and allow Him to empower them and to give them consistent victory - and to keep them from falling or sinning. God is no respecter of persons. He can give us the same victory.

No one who claims to be perfect is really perfect. Those who God sees as perfect are not aware of the fact, and are the last ones to boast of their own goodness or perfection, because the closer people get to God, the more they can see their nothingness and His greatness. The more they will be able to see just how perfect and loving God is and just how much they are lacking in perfection.

It is important to realize that temptation is not sin. Temptation is only the possibility to sin. Also, it is not a sin to have an evil thought. It only becomes a sin when we dwell on that thought and we lust after it, or desire to fulfill it.

Now I assure you that if God sees an individual as perfect they won't be boasting about being perfect, and they won't see themselves as being perfect. In fact, they will feel unworthy because the closer you get to God you will see just how imperfect and flawed you are in comparison to His perfection.

How Can We Overcome Sinning?

We can overcome sin by dying to self and to our old carnal, fleshly sin nature, being born again and partaking of the divine spiritual nature of Jesus and receiving the new *spiritual mind* of Christ. By yielding to the Holy Spirit and allowing Him to empower us to overcome sin. Also, by allowing Jesus to abide or live His life through us and control us by the power of His

Holy Spirit. But we have to yield because God does not force our will. We have to choose to obey. We have to allow Him to control us. We have to come to the point that we get so sick of sin until we hate it as God hates it with a perfect hatred. Let us never forget- God loves the sinner, but He hates sin. Sin and sinners will not enter heaven. If we could be saved in sin then Jesus wouldn't had to come and die for our sins.

The Bible says in Romans 6:6, that **"our old man (old sin nature) is to be crucified…**and Romans 11:6 says: **"Reckon, or (consider) yourselves to be dead to sin."** Galatians 2:20 says: **"I am crucified with Christ; nevertheless I live; yet not I, but Christ which liveth in me; and the life which I now live I live in the flesh I live by faith of the Son of God, who loved me, and gave Himself for me."** This is righteousness by faith. It means to be dead to self, but alive by Christ's life within us. It means to have faith that works by love, and to get to the point where you trust God explicitly whereby you become willing to give up your own life and by faith you allow Jesus to come and take over and live His life in and through you. The Bible say: **"Christ in you, the hope of Glory."** It is a mystery that Jesus comes and lives in us by the power of His Holy Spirit.

Unfortunately, some dear Christians have never experienced righteousness by faith. They have only experienced righteousness by works, which is self-righteousness, which is nothing but filthy rags. Some professed Christians have a legalistic religion. They try to do what is right by using their own strength – going about to establish their own righteousness, instead of allowing the righteousness of Christ's merits and life to control them.

It is the righteousness of Christ within us that saves. Jesus was our example and "**He was** *tempted* **in all points...yet without sin**" (Hebrews 4:15).

Jesus did *not* use His divine nature to help Him overcome temptation, because if He did He would have had an advantage over us, and therefore, could not be our perfect example. But Jesus had no advantage over us. The same heavenly Father that Jesus prayed to give Him the power to resist temptation and overcome sin is the same God we can pray to give us the power to resist temptation and overcome. The problem is that instead of people dying to self and yielding to God's power that is available to them to keep them from sinning; they are yielding to satan's power and yielding to his temptations. Jesus' death was our substitute. But His life was our example.

May Almighty God help us to determine to follow Jesus' example by turning from our sins and resisting temptation by asking God to give us the Holy Spirit and His grace to help us overcome as Christ overcame. Because according to Revelations chapters 2:7, Rev. 2:11, and 26, and Rev. 3: 5 and 12, only those who are the *"overcomers"* of sin will be able to enter heaven.

Sin is not a necessity. Sin is a *choice*! No sin or sinners will enter heaven. *The Christian life is one of daily surrender, and continual overcoming temptation and sin moment-by-moment. But only as he or she remains surrendered to the power of the Holy Spirit!*

As I stated earlier, by God's Amazing Grace, I have *overcome* the emotional issues that I used to try to only cope with. It wasn't the medication I took that set me free. It wasn't the counseling that healed me. Although, those things played an integral part in my recovery, however, ultimately, I must credit *God* for helping me to have the victory.

Some times when we are dealing with physical or emotional issues, we have a tendency to run to the doctor to get a drug, or go to a psychiatrist to get counseling. Yet, sadly, too often people overlook, or forget the *God-Factor*!

Some physical or emotional illnesses are not due to any physical problem, but stem from a spiritual problem. Some people simply need to get some sins out of their lives, and be born again and converted. And consequently, they would become new creatures in Christ Jesus. Some people need to die to their old, carnal, fleshly sin natures and become partakers of the divine, spiritual nature of Jesus Christ. Then they would get a new mind—a spiritual mind, which is the mind of Christ.

Once I confessed my sins to God and repented by turning away from my sins, and was born again, I no longer had depression, fear, worry, or guilt, because the mind of Christ that I had received does not have these problematic issues.

A major part of the mission of Christ is to get God's true children to bear the *fruits of the Holy Spirit in their character traits*, which are according to Galatians 5: 22, 23: love, peace, joy, patience, meekness, goodness, gentleness, faith, long-suffering, and self-control. Have you died to self so Jesus can live out His character in and through you so that your character reflects these traits?

Ask yourself: Are you loving, peaceful, joyful, gentle, patient, meek, have faith, willing to suffer long for Christ's sake, and have self-control, or temperance? If, not, please ask God to help you to reflect His character, and to give you His Holy Spirit so you can have a right spirit and bear the fruits of the Holy Spirit in your character traits.

Dear Beloved, Reader, allow me to leave you with these final thoughts.

If you're trying drugs to cope with any physical or emotional issues, that's fine. Also, if you're trying counseling to help you, well, that's okay too. But just don't forget to *try God*!

We can overcome our bad habits and wrong character traits by surrendering to the power of the Holy Spirit.

Some people are depressed because they do not understand the true definition of success. Therefore, they look upon their lives with despair, and as a complete failure.

I overcame fear and depression by the power of the Holy Spirit! Yield yourself totally to Him. You will be so glad that you totally surrendered your mind, your will, your wisdom, your body, your problems, your depression, your fears, your guilt, your worries, your enemies, your plans, and your *all* to Him! Because you could not be placing yourself in better hands than in the Omnipotent Hands of the Almighty!

I sincerely hope that this last poem blesses you.

The True Definition of Success!

Success does not depend on having fortune or
Fame.
True success is knowing God, and that He knows
Your name.
True success is giving God your best.
And daily growing in holiness.
True success is not living a life of luxury and
Ease.
But it's making God happy and pleased.

True Success is having Christ living within.
And daily overcoming the temptation to sin.
True success is doing right when no one is
Looking.
And living your life to be a blessing.
True success is speaking a kind word when
Someone needs it most.
And being filled with the Holy Ghost.
True success is being like Christ and living a
Righteous life.
And sleeping with a clean conscience at night.
True success is having peace of mind.
And trusting God even when you don't have a
Dime.
True success is not seeking this world's
Pleasures.
But seeking God's heavenly treasures.
True success is living a life of honesty.
And loving justice and mercy.
True success is doing God's holy will.
And forgiving your enemies and loving them
Still.
True success is to love instead of hate.
And to reflect God's image and character traits.
True success is being peaceful, loving, and kind.
And giving God quality time.
True success is being a soul-winner.
And being transformed into a saint from a sinner.
True success is to walk in truth and not in error.
And to have Christ as your Lord and Savior.

True success is to obey God's Holy Law.
And to serve and worship Him with reverence
And awe.
True success is not just living for yourself.
But doing good deeds for someone else.
True success is having all your debts paid.
And trusting God in all things and not being
Afraid.
True success is having your needs supplied.
And being truthful when you could have lied.
The true definition of success is not having the
Best that this world has to offer.
But it's reflecting God's love to one another,
And being worthy to live with *God forever!*

PLEASE READ THIS IMPORTANT MESSAGE!

If this book has been a blessing to you, please order additional copies for your loved ones, or please send a donation to help the author, Ruth Henderson to raise the funds to produce her next **evangelistic, soul-winning Poetry Concert?**

Ruth Henderson aka Ruth Truth is a gifted poet and what makes her so unique is that she uses God's Gift of Poetry to share the gospel, and she writes poems about unique topics that you would not expect a poem to address, such as: how to overcome depression and fear, or how to prosper, or the importance of witnessing!

You can also invite Ruth to your church or conference to recite her poetry, or to teach a physical and mental Health Workshop.

Ruth states, "Even though poetry is Biblical, it is rare to hear poetry in churches. I believe that God has called me to help *restore His Gift of Poetry* back to the church in these last days."

www.greatamericanpoetshow.org,

Order Form!

Email Orders: giftofpoetry1004@yahoo.com

On-line Orders: www.ruthhenderson.co

Postal Orders: Good News Publications
P.O. Box 831108
Stone Mountain, Georgia 30083

I want to order _____ copies of this book. I have enclosed my check or money order payable to: Ruth Henderson, and my payment of $12.95 per book and $2.00 shipping per book. Please **print** your info below!

Name: _____

Address: _____

Email: _____

Order Now!

THANK YOU FOR YOUR ORDER!

Bibliography

*All references that do not give the name of the authors were taken from books written by author, Ellen G. White, and published by the Review and Herald Publishing unless otherwise noted.

Note:
1. RH stands for Review and Herald Pub. Co.
2. DA stands for the book: Desire of Ages
3. TM stands for the book: Testimonies to Ministers
4. MH stands for the book: Ministry of Healing
5. SC stands for the book Steps to Christ
6. MCP stands for the book: Mind, Character, and Personality
7. GC stands for the book: The Great Controversy
8. Amazing Facts Publishing Study Guide 26, pp. 6, 7
9. HP stands for the book: Heavenly Places
10. COL stands for the book: Christ Object Lessons
11. GW stands for the book: Gospel Workers
12. MYP stands for the book: Messages to Young People 12

13. MB stands for the book: Thoughts From the Mount of Blessings
14. FILB stands for the book: Faith I Live By
15. Roger Morneau, Incredible Power of Prayer, p. 121 (1977), Review and Herald Pub.
16. FE stands for the book: Fundamentals of Christian Education
17. OHC stands for the book: Our High Calling
18. W.W. Prescott, Victory In Christ, pp. 12, 15, 16, Review and Herald Publishing (1987)
19. Council on Diet and Foods, p. 163, 167

www.ingramcontent.com/pod-product-compliance
Lightning Source LLC
LaVergne TN
LVHW021447080426
835509LV00018B/2196